.net Guide #3

All you need to know about
Using the Net

.net Guide #3

All you need to know about Using the Net

by Davey Winder

Future Publishing Limited
Beauford Court
30 Monmouth Street
Bath
Avon BA1 2BW

.net Guide #3 All you need to know about Using the Net

Future Publishing Limited, Beauford Court, 30 Monmouth Street, Bath, Avon BA1 2BW

ISBN 1-898275-33-5

British Library Cataloguing in Publication Data
A CIP catalogue record for this book is available from the British Library

Author Davey Winder

Series Editor Davey Winder

Book Editor Rod Lawton

Book Design Rod Lawton

Subbing and layout Janet Smith

Cover origination Nick Aspell

Printed and bound by Redwood Books

Contents

Dedication

This book is dedicated to my children, Nikita and Holly, who are the jewels in my crown.

Acknowledgements

The usual thanks to everyone concerned with the production of this book, including Rod Lawton and Ian Jones for actually having faith in the idea that there was a series of such books just waiting to be written, Yvonne for agreeing to marry me and making that one less thing to worry about, Simon "Lawny" Cooke and Karen "Howling Mad Kazza" Gentleman (yes her Mother is a Gentleman as well) for letting me let off steam at their house.

And a very special thank you to all the Internet Service Providers who have opened up the Internet to a UK audience – without them we would be going nowhere slowly.

About the author

Wavey Davey Winder has managed to carve out a name for himself as one of the UK's leading Internet experts in just a few short years. He is totally self taught when it comes to computers – they didn't have such things when he was at school. He has been described by a leading national newspaper as the "UK's first Virtual Celebrity" and the BBC introduced him as being "the UK's foremost guide to the Internet". Davey Winder is the author of a number of Internet and Comms related books, and writes for many different computer magazines. If you want to know anything about the Internet, but want the question answered in a way that you can actually understand, then Davey Winder is the right man for the job.

Books by the same author

'Internet, Modems, And The Whole Comms Thing', 'All You Need To Know About The Internet', 'All you need to know about Communicating On-Line', 'All you need to know about Mailing Lists', 'All you need to know about On-Line Gaming', 'All you need to know about UK Internet Service Providers', 'All you need to know about the World Wide Web', 'All you need to know about Business On-Line', 'All you need to know about Internet Jargon'.

How to use this book

.net Guide #3 All you need to know about Using the Net is one of a series of Internet books designed to focus on the needs of real Internet users.

For a full list of the books in this series – and details of other Internet publications we do – see the back of this book.

All of our Internet books are written in plain English for people who are more interested in the Net than computers. And to make it even easier, we've included icons in the margins to draw your attention to especially important pieces of information. Here are the icons, together with an explanation of what they mean (although it's all pretty obvious):

Make a note. Most of the things you read get stored away in your head somewhere or other. When you see this icon, though, make sure you store this particular item somewhere prominent. It's quite important.

Top Tip. There are lots of ways of saving time, money and effort that you'll never see in print. Except here!

What does it mean? Anything to do with the Internet is packed with jargon. You can't get rid of it, you just have to live with it. But that doesn't mean to say you can't explain it...

Warning! You won't see this icon too often, but when you do, pay attention! Ignoring it could cost you time, money or your sanity. And none of us have much to spare of any of those.

Chapter 1
Introduction

This book is designed to help those of you who have taken the plunge and got yourself an Internet account. This is the Hands-On Internet Reference, but don't think it is going to be beyond your understanding, I can assure you it won't be. It will advance your knowledge of the Net, letting you exploit the power of the resource before you fully. As well as looking at where the information you want is kept and giving you the directions to get there, this book will explain how to use the various applications and tools that make the Internet so powerful and useful.

You will learn how to use FTP to download files onto your desktop PC; how to browse the Internet for information using Gopher efficiently; how to connect to other computers and use their resources legally using Telnet; how to send an email message anywhere in the world; and how to find people on the Internet using Netfind and Whois.

You will discover who is protecting your interests as a user of the Internet, and how you can help them to help you. In this book you will find down to earth explanations of all the jargon you are likely to encounter on the Net, a smiley

The Internet. This image was downloaded from the Internet and you could find out how to get it from ftp.eff.org if you keep reading!

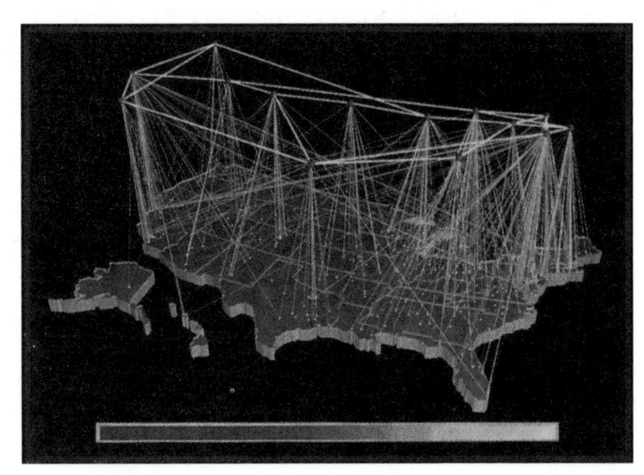

dictionary, an acronym dictionary, and a comprehensive glossary. A technical reference, too, will help to demystify such things as UNIX commands.

What you won't find in this book is coverage of email, Usenet, Internet Relay Chat, the World Wide Web, service providers, or how to get an Internet account up and running. Why? Because these subjects will all be covered in depth by other books in this series as they are of such importance to merit a volume all of their own. I won't abandon them completely though, and will tell you enough for you to decide if you want to find out more or not.

How does this book work?

Well, you open the pages and read them... OK, so you knew that. This book takes the format of a guided tour of the Internet, a road map of the Infobahn, which will stop off at various places along the way to show you what can be done and how to do it. The different tools and applications of the Internet will be explained, with help on their usage and handy command reference guides. An extremely useful Internet Resource Directory can be found at the back of the book to point you in the direction of specific resources and areas of interest. Throughout the book icons will be used to help you locate items such as tips, expert help, and so on.

One thing that doesn't matter is what type of computer you are using to get onto the Internet, it could be an Amiga, PC, Macintosh, Atari, or anything else that allows serial communications. The Internet doesn't care what computer platform you use, and to be honest, neither does this book.

Screenshots may appear to favour one platform and there is a good reason for this, it is what I used to compile the book!

What is the Internet?

The Internet is a world-wide network of computer networks, more than three million of them in fact, with an estimated 30 million users. You can forget about the computers for a moment, because the Internet is a concept, a tool, the most powerful communications resource the world has ever seen.

It is used for a host of different purposes, by a host of equally different people. You can search for information, send electronic mail across the globe in an instant, download the latest shareware and public domain programs, make new friends anywhere in the world, research your school or business project, keep an eye on the latest news, do your shopping, get technical information, run your business, you can even play chess with an opponent in America if you want.

The type of people using the Internet are not the stereotypical computer geeks and scientists you may imagine either; there are government departments, universities, large corporations, commercial on-line services, and every type of individual from bikers to businessmen, pilots to policemen, and housewives to house builders.

As I've already mentioned, this book assumes you already have an Internet account. if you haven't, then you will need the service of a company that can provide you with one. There are a growing number of Internet service providers in the UK. These range from dedicated services that exist just to get you Internet connected, through to the big commercial on-line systems which offer their users Internet access as part of a much bigger package.

The choice is yours and I would recommend you read the book in this series that is devoted to service providers to help you make the choice. However, to get you started here are contact numbers that will enable you to get more information from just some of these companies themselves:

BBC Networking Club	081 993 6281
CityScape Internet Services Ltd	0223 566950
Compulink Information eXchange (CIX)	081 390 8446
Delphi	071 757 7150
Demon Internet Ltd	081 349 0063
Direct Connection	081 317 0100
EasyNet	071 209 0990
EUNet GB	0227 266466
ExNet	081 244 0077
PC User Group	081 863 1191
Pipex Ltd	0223 250120
SoNet	0703 397518

The Internet outline

This chapter will give you a brief outline of what the Internet can offer in the way of resources. The main areas of use can be broken down into five categories:

- Electronic mail
- Information browsing
- File transfer

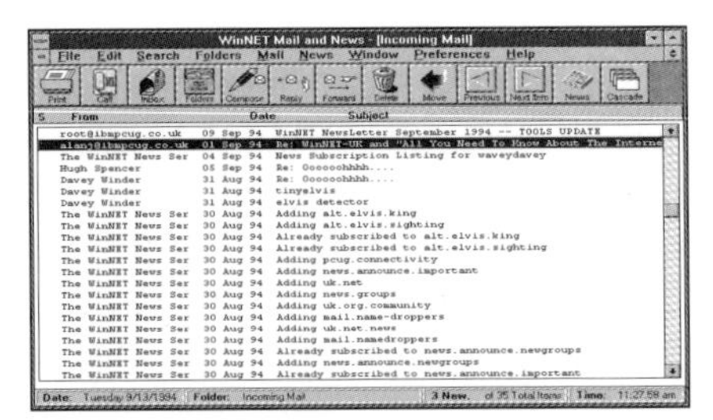

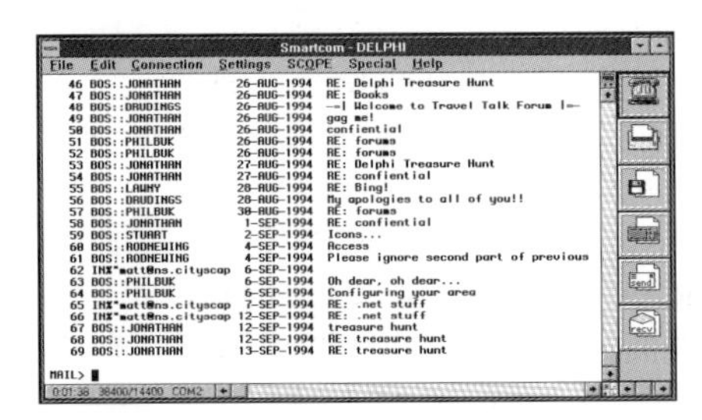

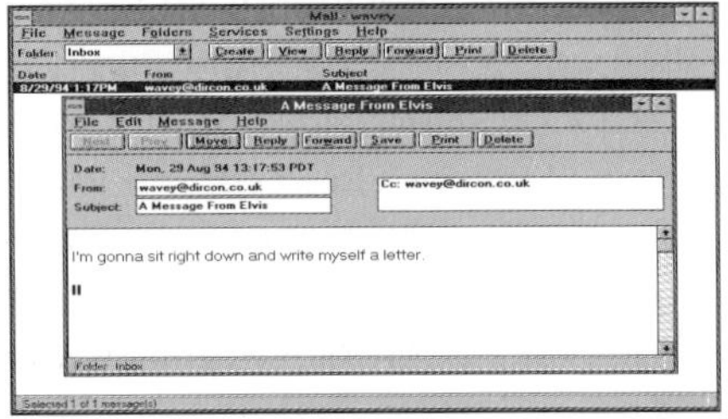

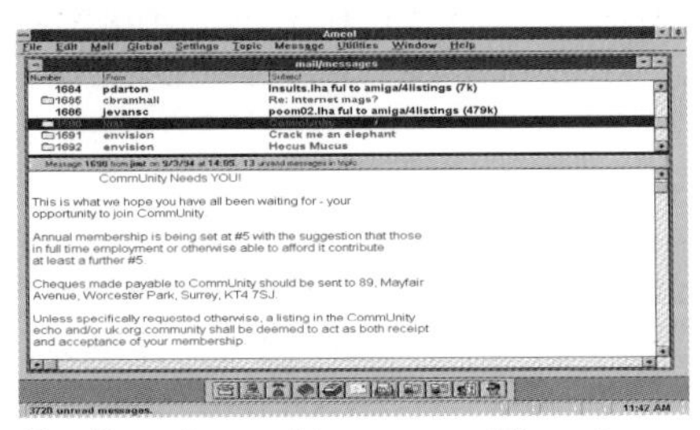

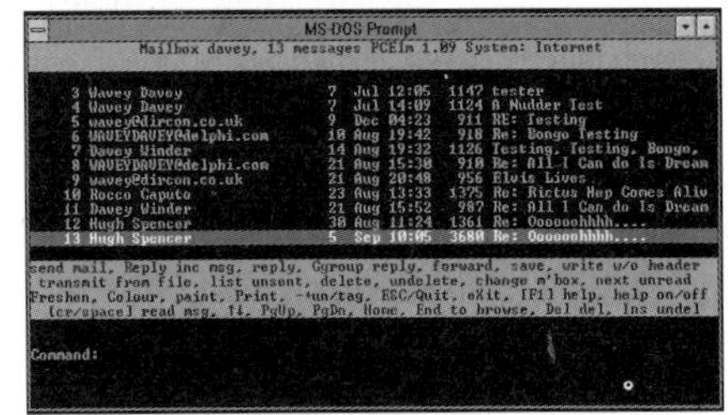

Email can be read in a many different ways, as you can see here.

- Using other computers
- Socialising

Electronic mail is probably the first thing you think of when someone mentions computer communications, it is probably the most used application on the Internet too. Not surprisingly so, after all, why wait days for your post to get delivered when you can send it safely in seconds anywhere in the world using the Internet? With email you aren't restricted to just sending text either, you can use simple tools to attach pictures, sounds, even video to your messages. It's fast, efficient, cost effective, and if you don't have an electronic mailbox you might just be missing out on a business or social opportunity!

Computers are good are storing, sorting, and searching for information. A computer network makes this an even more useful ability, the Internet makes it an amazingly powerful resource. Information browsing already accounts for a large percentage of Internet use. With the arrival of more powerful and, importantly, simpler to use search and retrieval tools, this aspect of using the Internet could grow even bigger. Archie and Gopher let you search the whole of the Internet for specific files, documents, pictures, sounds, in fact just about any information that can be found in cyberspace.

The World Wide Web brings all this information even closer, using a method of hypertext documents to link the information together. Using the World Wide Web with one of the graphical browser programs which are now available transforms the Internet into a sprawling, colourful, lively,

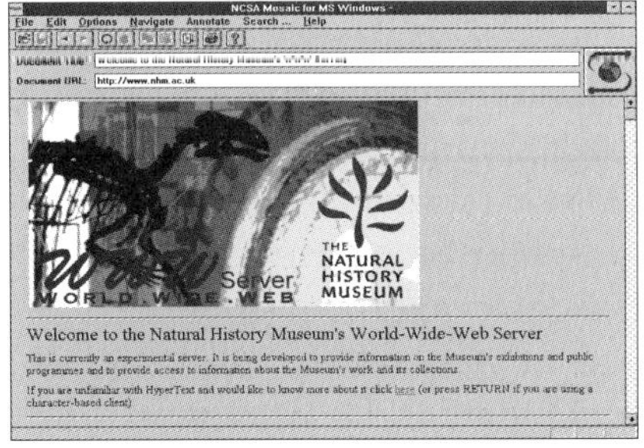

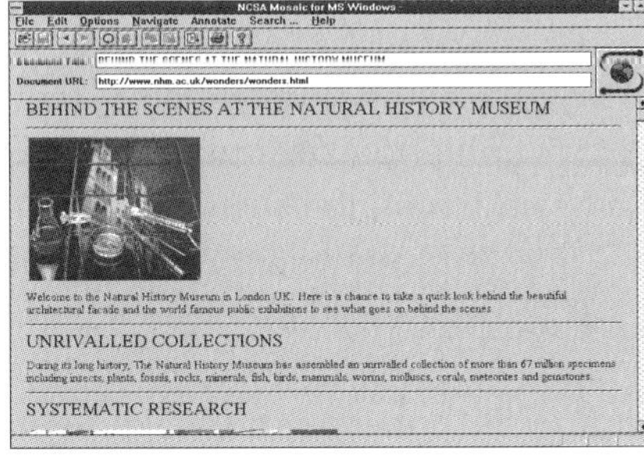

World Wide Web, the eighth wonder of the world?

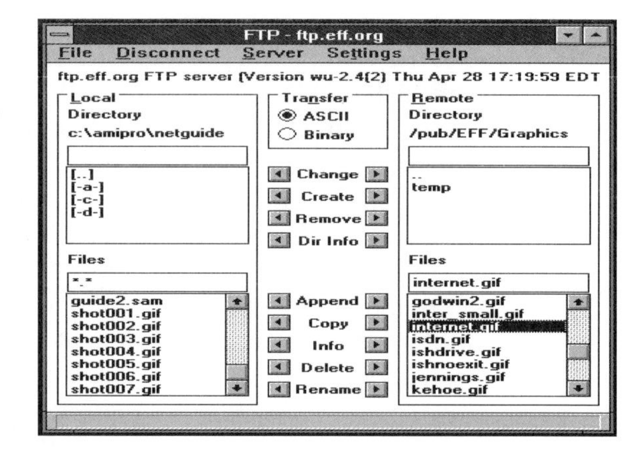

Moving files around the Internet isn't a problem, they could just as easily be on a computer in the next room or one in Japan, it really makes no difference.

interactive and immensely informative magazine on your computer screen.

Considering the amount of information to choose from, it would be more surprising than Elvis making a comeback if you didn't want to download some files to your computer at some point. The Internet has an easy method of doing this, known as FTP. There are hundreds of sites around the Internet where shareware and public domain software, which allow anyone to access them, are just waiting for you to pop in and take your pick. It would be true to say that the Internet is, in fact, the World's largest shareware library. It certainly has the longest opening hours!

Many companies are now using the Internet as a method of distributing upgrades for their software, I send the magazine articles I write (with accompanying pictures) to my editors using the Internet, and people are moving Gigabytes of information this way every single day of the year.

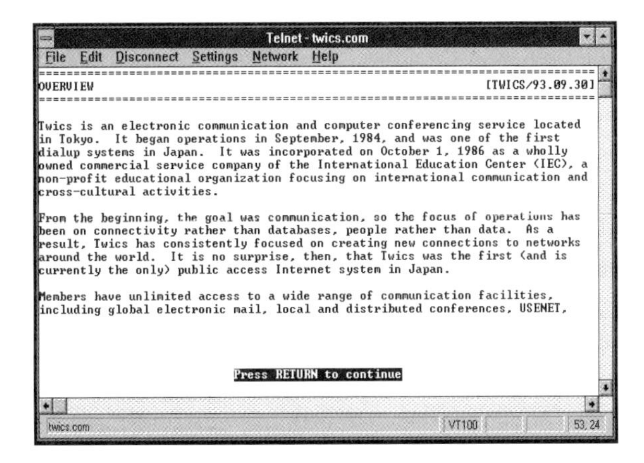

Using Telnet to connect to far off computers and on-line systems saves time and money.

I've already explained that the Internet is: a global network of computer networks. So it would be a bit pointless if you couldn't connect to other networks and computers using it. Luckily you can, with an Internet application called Telnet, but don't start thinking this all sounds a little bit dodgy and dangerous. Rest assured, nobody can creep into your computer and remove all your top secret files from your hard disk, you can only connect to computers that you have authorised access to, or that allow open access to anyone.

By now I hope you will have started to get the idea that the Internet is a useful resource for personal use and for business, but that doesn't mean you can't have fun as well. Those 30 million users do get together and talk to each other, although not all at the same time I'm glad to say.

Socialising using the Internet is something of a phenomenon, not only do people have serious debates over current issues, but they also chat just like they do at a party or in the pub, they argue, they fall in love, and some even get married after courting over the Internet.

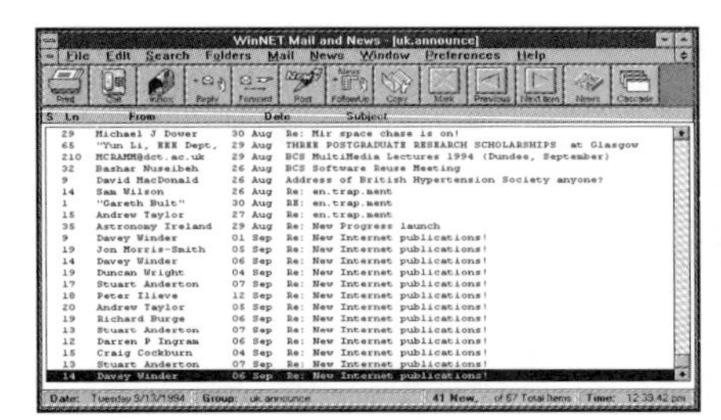

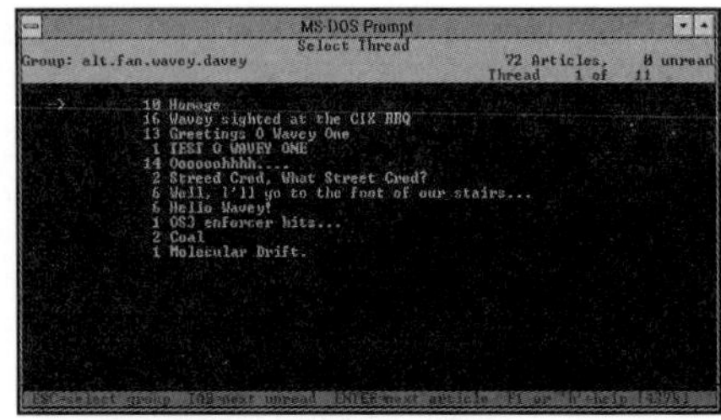

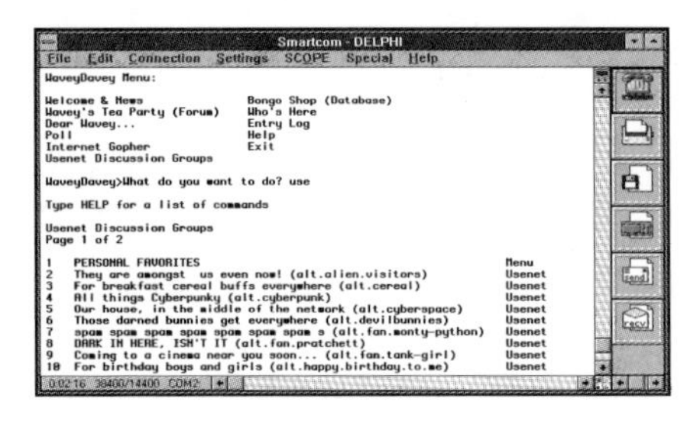

Just some of the programs that help make Usenet News easy to read and compile.

Usenet is the most popular method of social contact and discussion, and comprises a network of discussion groups that are fed by email contributions. There are more than 7,000 of these "Newsgroups" and they cover every conceivable subject matter. You can even talk in real time to other Internet users, anywhere in the world, using a tool called Internet Relay Chat.

OK, so now you know something of the Internet's specification, I bet you want to get under the hood and get your hands dirty, so to speak. So jump in and join me on a test drive down the Information Superhighway.

Chapter 2
Electronic mail

Email is simply the process of sending a private message using computers instead of the traditional postal services using pen and paper. Because of the comparative slowness of sending a letter by traditional means this type of postal service has become known to the on-line fraternity as "snail mail".

You may think this a bit harsh, after all a letter sent by first class post usually arrives the next day, maybe two or three days for overseas mail, that's not bad is it? OK, now compare that to sending a letter by email which takes a few seconds, and that's a few seconds anywhere in the world!

Oh, and when I say a letter, that letter can contain more than words (I'll start singing in a moment folks). It is possible, and practical, to send images, sounds, and binary code by email.

Using something like UUencode to convert the binary code to a text-based format is simple these days, and with the arrival of new standards such as MIME (Multi-purpose Internet Mail Extensions) this is becoming ever more useful. Imagine, you could send a business client an email message about some aspect of your company and attach a spreadsheet file, or database file, or even an animation or video to your letter.

So it is a pretty cool way of communicating, but what are the tangible advantages of email over and above sending an ordinary letter through the post, or making a telephone call?

- **Speed**
  Email is fast. Very fast.

- **Cost**
  Email is cheap. It costs the same to send a message to Hong Kong as it does to Blackpool.

- **Efficiency**
  Sending courtesy copies is simple, sending bulk mail outs is simple, forwarding email is simple.

What's in an address?

If you are unsure what a person's username is, but know the rest of the email address, then try sending a message requesting further information addressed to the postmaster there. For example, if you knew you could find me at wavey.demon.co.uk, but didn't know my username, you could send a message to:
`postmaster@wavey.demon.co.uk`

Hey, good question! For email to stand any chance of arriving at its destination it must be addressed properly, in the same way you need to ensure you put the correct address label on a letter when you post it. email addresses may look complicated, but they are similar in concept to any other form of address. Let's break one down and take a look.

One of my email addresses is:

`wavey@dircon.co.uk`

This can be seen as being two parts, my name is before the @ separator and my address is after it. In Internet terms the second part of the email address, the part after the @ separator, is known as a domain. In this example, dircon is the name of the service provider I am using, co means that it is a company, and uk tells us that it is based in the United Kingdom. So if you were to read that email address from right to left you would see that it starts off by being in the UK, then it tells us we are looking for a company, that the company is on a host computer called dircon, and that the person the email is intended for is wavey. There, that wasn't difficult, was it?

email addresses vary wildly in content, but they all follow the same standard structure. There are numerous country codes and organisational codes that you may come across, so to make this a bit clearer here is a guide to what are known as "top level domain codes".

Top level domain country codes

Code	Country
aq	Antarctica
ar	Argentina
at	Austria
au	Australia
be	Belgium
br	Brazil
ca	Canada
ch	Switzerland
cl	Chile
cr	Costa Rica
cs	Czechoslovakia
cy	Cyprus
de	Germany
dk	Denmark

ec	Ecuador
ee	Estonia
es	Spain
fi	Finland
fr	France
gl	Greenland
gr	Greece
hk	Hong Kong
hr	Croatia
hu	Hungary
ie	Ireland
il	Israel
in	India
is	Iceland
it	Italy
jp	Japan
kr	Korea (Republic of)
kw	Kuwait
lu	Luxembourg
lv	Latvia
mx	Mexico
my	Malaysia
nt	Netherlands
no	Norway
nz	New Zealand
pl	Poland
pr	Puerto Rico
pt	Portugal
ru	Russian Federation
se	Sweden
sg	Singapore
sk	Slovakia
sl	Slovenia
th	Thailand

tn	Tunisia
tr	Turkey
tw	Taiwan
uk	United Kingdom
us	United States
ve	Venezuela
za	South Africa

Top level domain organisation codes

com	Commercial organisation
edu	Educational facility
gov	Non-military government bodies
mil	Military concerns
org	Other organisations
net	Network resources

When you get some email you may notice there appears to be an awful lot of garbage at the start of the message, although you may not see it, as many mail programs hide this from the user. However, this stuff isn't garbage at all,

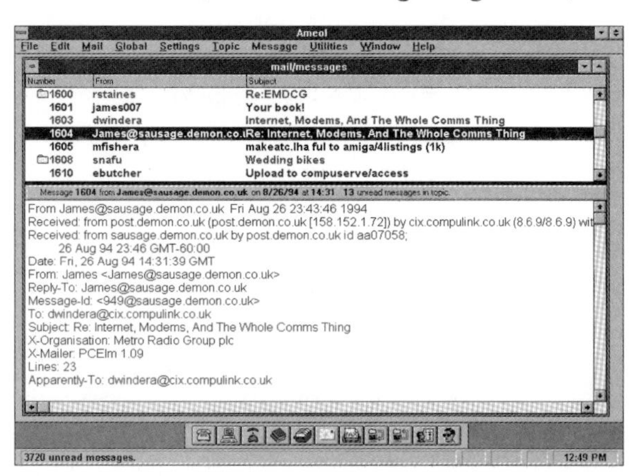

Email headers may look like rubbish, but, in fact, they are a treasure trove of useful information.

but important information about the email and the route it has taken to reach you, it's known as an email header.

If you send a letter by snail mail, and it doesn't get delivered, often it will come back to you with writing on the envelope detailing why it didn't make it. The postman may have noted that he couldn't find the address, for example. With email that's what a header relates to. All the postman's scribble is written in it so you can see exactly what route the message took to get to you, or not as the case may be.

An email header also contains information about the message itself, such as who it is addressed to, if any courtesy copies should be sent, the time it was sent, and so on. All in all, pretty useful garbage! Having said all that though, there is no need to see an email header unless something has gone wrong and you want to try and trace the problem, so let your mail program continue to hide them from you for the time being.

Internet phone book

One area of electronic mail that can be seen as a negative aspect is the difficulty involved in finding someone's email address if you don't already know it. It is easy if you want to send a letter, or make a phone call, to someone by traditional methods as you just consult the phone book, *Yellow Pages*, or directory enquiries. The Internet is a different kettle of slimy things with scales and tails, however. With more than 30 million people connected to the Internet, and another one million joining them on a monthly basis, you can imagine that compiling a

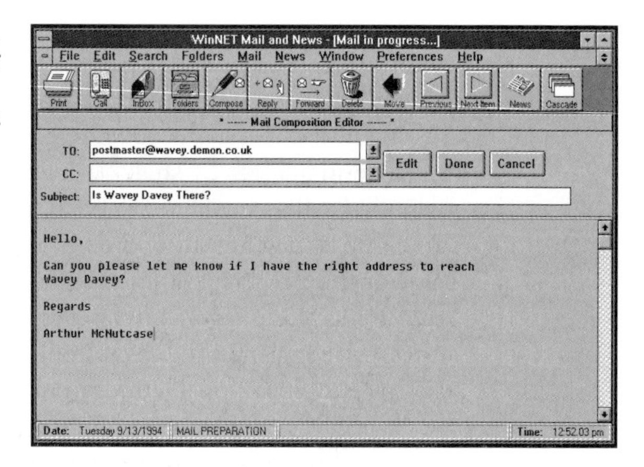

Sending an enquiry off to a postmaster, always be brief and polite if you want to stand any chance of a reply.

directory of names and addresses would be a mammoth task, in fact, nearly impossible.

There are, however, a few options open to you in trying to track down an email address. First, if you know the site where the person is then you can always send email to the postmaster there and ask for help. This doesn't always work, but is certainly worth trying. Second, there are a number of databases and searching tools available on the Internet that will help you with your quest, the degree of success varies wildly, and many of them, not unexpectedly, have a USA bias. The following are the most popular and useful:

Finger

Finger is an easy way of checking to see if the address you have is the right one for someone you are looking for, and can return information about that person and their account. The information that gets displayed when you "finger" someone can include the contents of a file called a plan file if that person has one. This can act as a mini-resumé, or even hold greater information. Many sites use finger and plan files as a way of distributing information, try fingering the following address for news from NASA, for example:

```
nasanews@space.mit.edu
```

However, it does have its drawbacks. For a start, you need to know a fair bit about the address you are looking for if Finger is going to be any use to you as an address searching tool. Not all systems support the Finger command, for example Delphi disables this command on grounds of user privacy. Not all users have plan files, or may just have empty ones, so limited information may get returned. Finally, if you finger a common name in your search for a specific account, then you may well get screen upon screen of information about every single user with that name!

Most service providers support the finger command, and you should be able to use it just by typing:

```
finger <name>@<address>
```

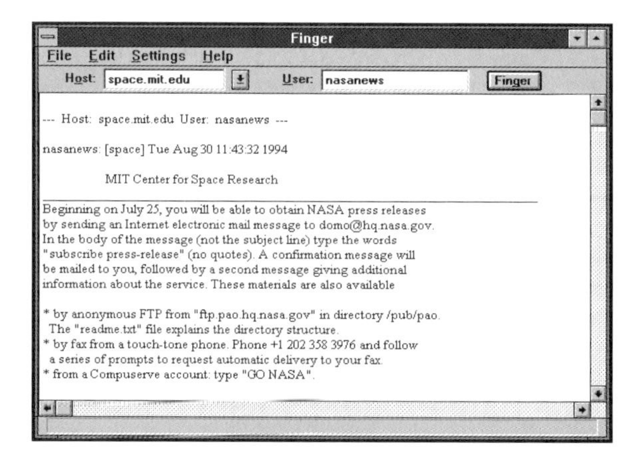

The NASA news report in finger format!

I've already mentioned using Finger to access information such as that held at NASA. However, there has been an explosion of a rather odd use of this feature in the past few years. Many university sites in the United States have drink dispensing machines connected to the Internet! Yep, only in America huh? Anyway, you can finger a coke machine and find out how many cans it contains, how much change is in it, when it was last used, even the temperature of the Coke. Apparently this all started when some students got fed up walking to the machine from their rooms only to find it was empty, or they didn't have the required change. Nice to see the Internet being used for a practical, useful, and important purpose...

If you want to finger a coke machine try any of the following addresses:
cocacola@columbia.edu
coke@cmu.edu
coke@cs.wisc.edu
coke@xcf.berkeley.edu
info@drink.csh.rit.edu

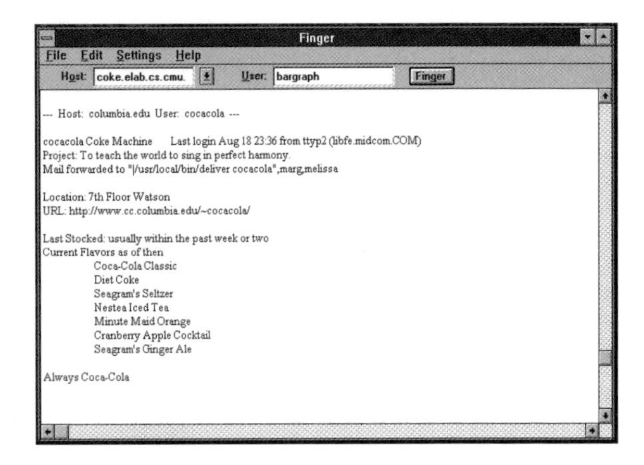

A finger of fun from the Internet.

Using NetFind at Imperial College is really easy, if you get stuck you just ask for help!

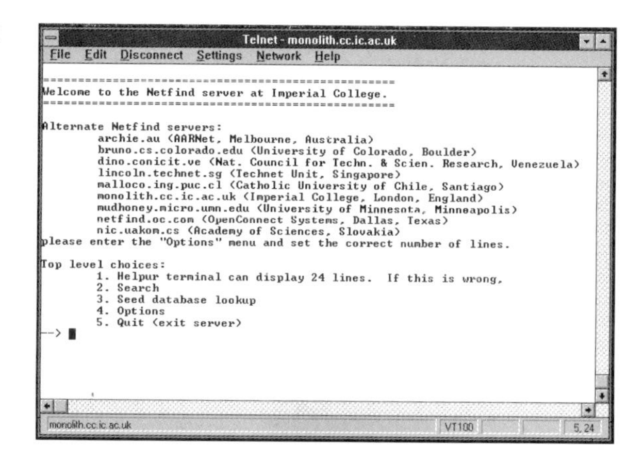
Telnet - monolith.cc.ic.ac.uk
File Edit Disconnect Settings Network Help
Welcome to the Netfind server at Imperial College.
Alternate Netfind servers:
archie.au (AARNet, Melbourne, Australia)
bruno.cs.colorado.edu (University of Colorado, Boulder)
dino.conicit.ve (Nat. Council for Techn. & Scien. Research, Venezuela)
lincoln.technet.sg (Technet Unit, Singapore)
malloco.ing.puc.cl (Catholic University of Chile, Santiago)
monolith.cc.ic.ac.uk (Imperial College, London, England)
mudhoney.micro.umn.edu (University of Minnesota, Minneapolis)
netfind.oc.com (OpenConnect Systems, Dallas, Texas)
nic.uakom.cs (Academy of Sciences, Slovakia)
please enter the "Options" menu and set the correct number of lines.
Top level choices:
1. Helpur terminal can display 24 lines. If this is wrong,
2. Search
3. Seed database lookup
4. Options
5. Quit (exit server)
-->
monolith.cc.ic.ac.uk
VT100
5, 24

NetFind

NetFind was developed by Mike Schwarz of Colorado University, and helps locate people on the Internet by searching a number of databases. However, because there are so few of these databases available, and those that are, are often not very comprehensive, a NetFind search may not be successful.

NetFind works by asking you to specify the first or last name of the person you want to find, followed by a number of keys. These keys take the form of the country where the person is located, place of work and so on. The more information you can give, the more successful your search is likely to be. If I was trying to find someone by the name of Billy Bongo who worked in the computer department of Imperial College, I would use a NetFind query of:

```
netfind bongo Imperial College computing
```

Currently, there are a number of NetFInd gateways on Gopher servers, or you can always Telnet to a NetFind client such as the one at Imperial College in the UK, using netfind as the login name. The address of the Imperial College NetFind client is:

`monolith.cc.ic.ac.uk`

Other sites which you can telnet to include:

`bruno.cs.colorado.edu`
`ds.internic.net`
`mudhoney.micro.umn.edu`
`netfind.oc.com`
`redmont.cis.uab.edu`

WHOIS

Perhaps the largest database of Internet organisations and users is located at the InterNic Registration Services host at **`rs.internic.net`**. You can search this database using WHOIS to return detailed information.

Unfortunately, this will be restricted mainly to network administrators and organisations as that is what the InterNic database holds details of. However, as more and more

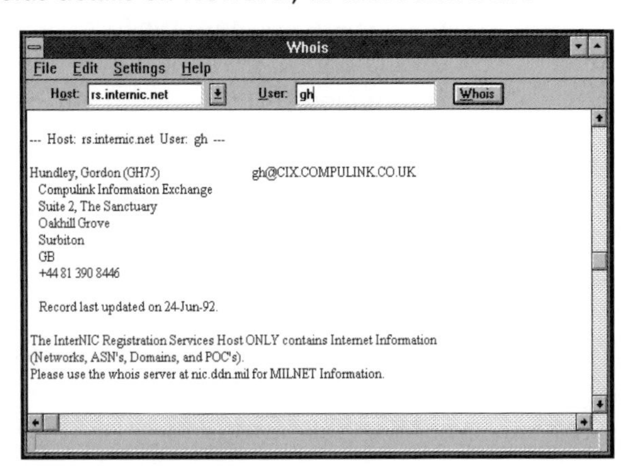

A typical WHOIS search.

details are added to the database then WHOIS could become an even more useful tool than it is now.

Chapter 3
Information browsing

While the Internet is undoubtedly an incredible information resource, finding the information you want could be a bit like looking for a small pointy metal thing in a big pile of dried grass. I say could be, as there are a number of Internet applications that make the job not only a whole lot easier, but in some cases, an absolute pleasure. Let's take a look at them.

Gopher

As well as being a north American burrowing rodent, the mascot of the University of Minnesota, and a type of tortoise, a Gopher is also one of the most valuable Internet applications you will come across. Developed by a team at the University of Minnesota, hence its name, the Internet Gopher presents the user with a simple menu-driven method of navigating through the Internet. One shouldn't really talk about the Internet Gopher as if there is only one,

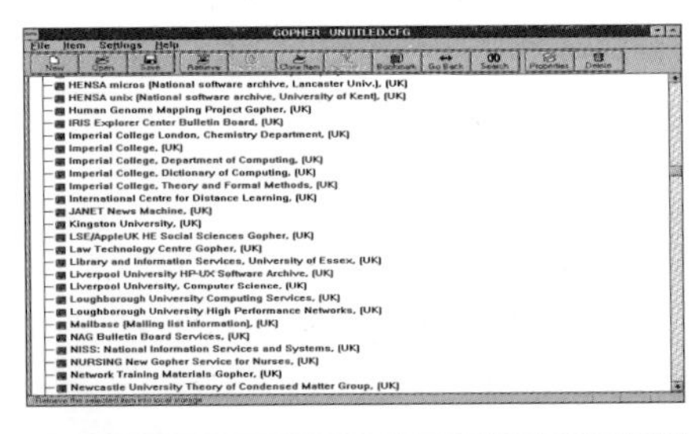

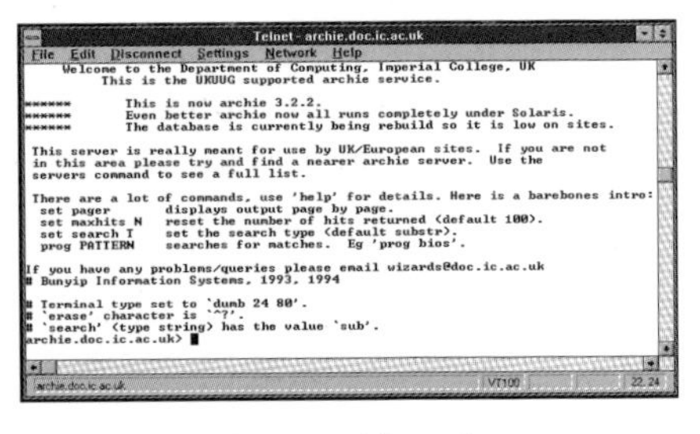

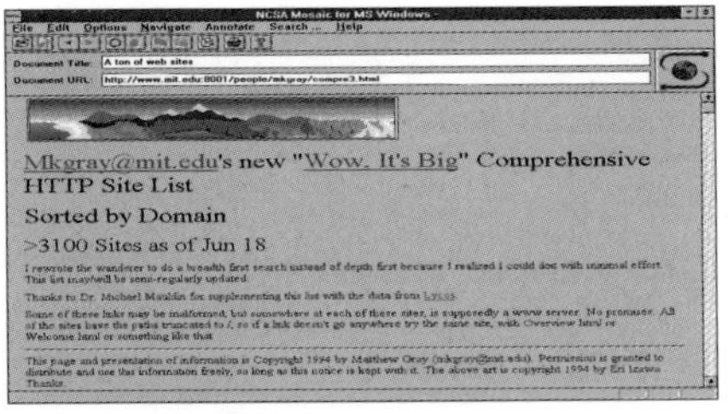

The Internet is something of an information jungle, luckily there are plenty of tools to help get you through it.

in fact there are hundreds of Gopher servers and thousands of Gopher clients.

Clients and servers operate all over the Internet, and together they work to help make your life much easier. A server is a computer that performs a task for another computer, a client is the computer that makes that request.

Generally, the client has a friendly front end so things are as simple as possible for the person using it, it really doesn't care about how the server does its job as long as it does. The server does all the donkey work; connecting to other computers and generally being technical. The important thing is that it delivers the requested information to the client who can then present it to the user.

Client and server operations are helping to make the Internet a user friendly place, you can tell your client program to do something with just a mouse click or two and you don't have to worry about how complex performing that task is for the server.

Using Gopher you can search for information, download documents, connect to other computers, link to Usenet Newsgroups, all from a straightforward menu system.

Without even realising it, every time you make a selection from a Gopher menu you are connecting to another computer or network, it could be on the other side of the planet, transferring information for you to browse through. This is known as Gopherspace, and you burrow through it searching for the information you require.

Gopher only opens a connection to another computer long enough to send a request for information, it then closes the connection until the requested data is ready and then opens it again to receive the reply. This saves on valuable network resources, and at the same time gives the user a really easy way of driving down the Infobahn.

Some Gophers don't contain any files themselves, but just act as links to other Gophers. The menu items on a Gopher may be gateways to a Telnet session, or a search for information using a keyword. However, many Gophers contain information in the form of files, which may be text, sound, a binary file and so on. Each menu item, be it a gateway or a file, has an identifier which you will not normally see as the Gopher client hides them out of view. Sometimes you may want to request information about an item, and then you will be faced with an "identifier" with no explanation of what it means! To help you out I have put together a quick and dirty guide to Gopher identifiers:

Menu Type	**Identifier**
Archived File (DOS)	5
Binary File	9
BinHexed File (MAC)	4
Directory	1
Error	3
File	0
Image File (GIF)	g
Image File	i
Index Search	7
MIME email file	M
Phonebook Server	2
Sound File	s

Telnet Session	8
Telnet 3270 Session	T
UUencoded File	6

To make matters complicated, not all Gopher clients can view all these different file types. For example, the standard "text and cursor" type of Gopher can only handle text files. Trying to view a file type not handled by your Gopher client is a waste of time and may crash your computer. So make sure you know what type of files your Gopher can handle before you start using it, which may involve (goodness forbid) reading the documentation!

Wherever possible use a Gopher client rather than connecting by Telnet. A client is usually much faster. A Telnet connection to a Gopher may end up in extremely slow response times due to the heavy loads that Gophers experience.

There are many different types of Gopher clients available, most service providers will have a Gopher client of the "text and cursor" type. This is a simple character-based Gopher client and is a capable and adequate tool for the job. If your service provider doesn't have a Gopher client on hand, then you can use the Mother of all Gophers at Minnesota (birthplace of the Gopher) by Telnetting to:

```
consultant.micro.umn.edu
```

Use "gopher" as your login, and then follow the easy instructions to make use of your very own Internet Librarian.

You will find there are lots of commands that are available when using a character-based Gopher client. Although most of the navigating can be accomplished using menu item selection you may find the following commands useful:

Gopher commands

Navigating Gopherspace

Use the following arrow keys to move around, and then just press return when you want to look at a document.

Up	Move to previous line
Down	Move to next line
Right	Select current item
Left	Exit current item
> **or** +	View next page
< **or** -	View previous page
m	Return to main menu

You don't need to press "enter" while at the Gopher menus, just typing in the commands as shown is enough.

Bookmark commands

Bookmarks are used to pinpoint interesting places on your travels, rather than going through all the menu options you had to first time around. In effect, what you end up with is your own personalised Gopher menu. Not all Gopher clients support this feature, so make sure yours does!

a	Add the current item to the bookmark list
A	Add the current directory or search to the bookmark list
v	View the bookmark list
d	Delete a bookmark from the list

A graphical Gopher makes the going even (damn, can't think of another 'G' word) better.

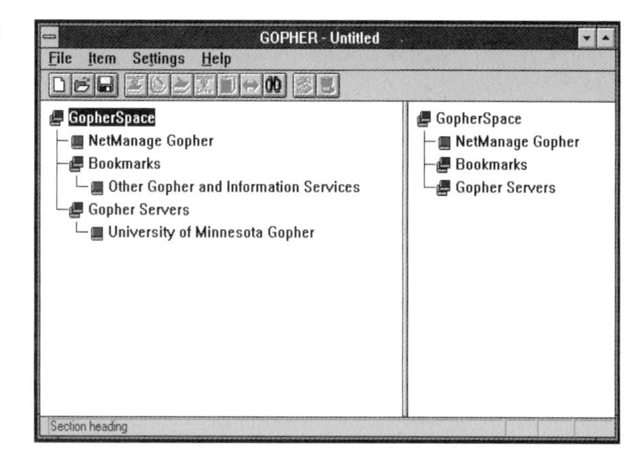

Other useful Gopher commands

D Download a file
n Find next search item
O Change your options

q Quit (with confirmation)
Q Quit (no confirmation)
s Save current item to a file
= Display information about current item
/ Search for a menu item

Watch out for Gopher+ servers which are starting to appear and offer the ability to retrieve formatted text versions of the same document. So one document could be available in PostScript, Microsoft Word, Rich Text Format, and plain ASCII. The team at the University of Minnesota is also working on support for on-line forms. This will allow such resources as on-line conferencing systems, databases and much more to be attached to Gophers.

While "text and cursor" Gopher clients are fully functional and certainly not lacking in power, they are hardly state of the art when it comes to looking good. To get a good looking Gopher that gives you an even more intuitive interface and exploits fully the power of the Gopher resource, then you should look at one of the graphical Gopher clients that are starting to appear.

A couple are available for Windows users already, and I'm sure that other platforms will follow suit before long (probably before this book is even published). I use a graphical Gopher these days, and find it has many advantages, including:

- Ease of use, no command sets to learn, just point and click. It is no more difficult than using a directory utility.
- The Windows clients let you set up file associations so different file types are recognised and acted upon automatically. So a text file will get viewed through a text editor, and an image will go through an image viewer and so on.
- Breathes extra life into a Gopher by introducing the elements of sound and vision.

There is a slight problem with Gophers, and that is that more and more have appeared on the Internet making the task of searching through them all time consuming. In fact, you may say you need a Gopher to get through all the Gophers, let alone the Internet that lies beyond.

However, an application called Veronica is at hand to save the day, and maybe even the whole week. Veronica works in much the same way as a Gopher, but keeps an index of Gopher items that allow keyword searches of the titles they hold. If you were to enter the word "Internet" then Veronica would return a menu of hundreds of Gopher menu items that contain that keyword.

To connect to the Gopher that looks of interest you just select the relevant item from the Veronica menu. The majority of Gophers now have an item on their main menu which is marked as Veronica, so try it out as I think you will find her to be a most useful addition to the burrowing rodent family.

Wide Area Information Servers

Wide Area Information Servers are usually referred to by the acronym WAIS. This tool differs from Gopher as it allows you to search for text contained within documents such as FAQ files, Usenet Newsgroups and text files, rather than just the name of a file or directory. WAIS will let you search for specific information from many different databases, held at various locations. Because there are thousands of different databases holding textual information spread over the

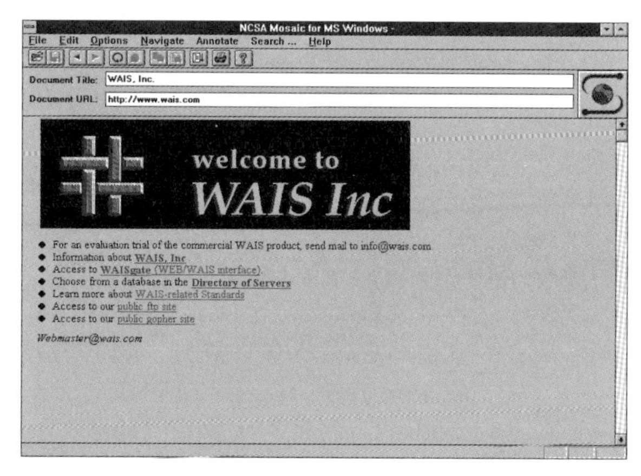

WAIS as seen from the World Wide Web, this site can be found at `http://www.wais.com`

Internet, there are also a whole bucketful of different searching methods for performing searches of them. WAIS tidies this up for you and lets you search these differing databases using the one single, simple, interface.

Because WAIS is searching for a keyword in maybe millions of other words, it can take a while to perform a search and get the results back to you. The more specific you are in your set of keywords to search, the better the chances of getting a good match to your needs. WAIS cannot perform Boolean searches, which let you use AND, IF, and OR statements within your search criteria. For example, if you ask WAIS to search for WAVEY AND BALLERINA it will find all the documents containing the words WAVEY, BALLERINA, and AND, rather than documents only containing both WAVEY and BALLERINA together.

WAIS is still a pretty damn clever application in other aspects though. Like providing each document in the list it returns with a score out of 1,000 depending on how closely it matches your requirements. Or how about a feature called "relevance feedback" which lets you mark the documents in the list that you feel are most relevant to your needs. WAIS then looks for other documents that are similar to those ones. By using the relevance feedback system you can get specific and useful documents, although this procedure can take an awfully long time.

The World Wide Web

The World Wide Web, or WWW for short, is a hypertext-based, information browsing tool. Sounds pretty dull doesn't it? How about if I said it was a massive, world-wide,

The World Wide Web is like the biggest CD-ROM you are ever likely to encounter!

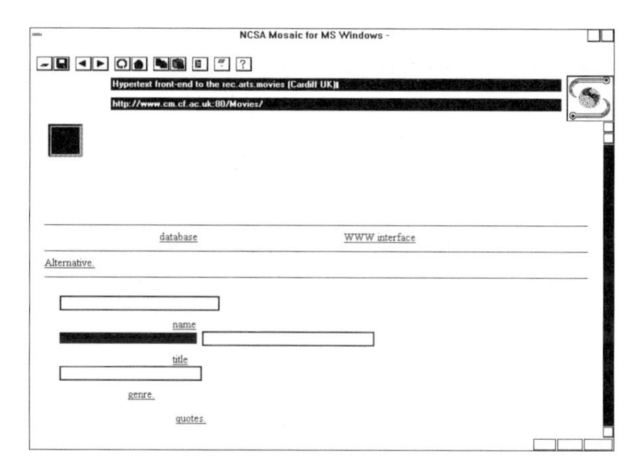

interactive magazine which brings the power of the Internet to your desktop in an attractive, intuitive, and totally addictive package.

That sounds a bit more exciting, but even that cannot do the Web justice. You really do have to use it to appreciate its power and understand why WWW is such an important Internet resource. Not only does the World Wide Web make exploration of the Internet child's play, my five and six-year-old daughters are proof of that, but it makes it fun too!

WWW was developed at the European Laboratory for Particle Physics in Switzerland (known as CERN) as recently as 1990, and uses a system of documents which contain hypertext links within them. Using something called HyperText Mark-up Language (HTML), documents have embedded hypertext links which enable the user to jump from one piece of information to another related item at the click of a mouse button. These "jumps" can be to different pages in the same document, to other documents held at the same site, or to documents held on different computers anywhere in the world. The information in these documents

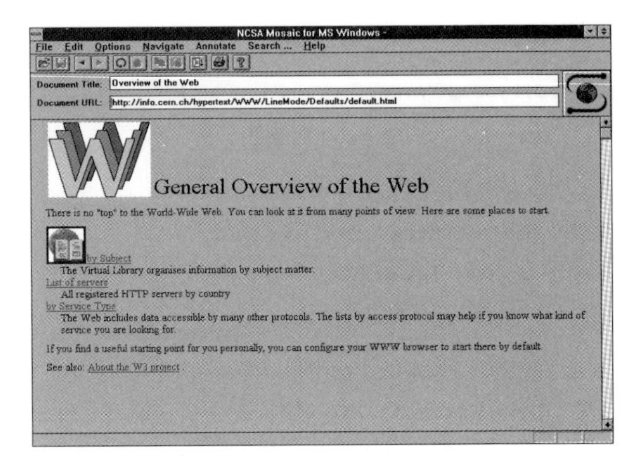

The home of the World Wide Web, CERN, as seen from the Web itself.

isn't restricted to just text either, but can be a mixture of text, sound, image, and even video.

To help explain the principle, imagine you have a page of a magazine open in front of you, there is an article about the 1950s you are reading. You see a reference to cars of the period, press the word "car" and the page changes to present you with an article about 1950s cars. After reading that you go back to your original, or home, page and see a picture of Elvis, press the picture and you hear an Elvis song. You see a reference to some news events, select that and the page turns into a video screen showing newsreel film of the time. If you can imagine that, then you have grasped the reality of the World Wide Web. It's like the biggest CD-ROM you are ever likely to encounter!

You can connect to the Web either by using a character-based client which will be available from most service providers, or you could Telnet to a site that has such a client. However, by far the best way to exploit the power of WWW is to use a graphical browser, for which you need a direct, dial-in, Internet account. The most popular graphical

browser is, without any shadow of a doubt, a program called Mosaic which I'll come back to in a moment.

If you are using a service such as Cix or Delphi for your Internet access, or are Telnetting to a site that has a WWW client, then you will be using a character-based browser. This is the easiest option as the client has been set up and is ready for you to use, but there are a number of commands that you will need to learn, and you don't get to see the graphical side of the Web which really is a shame.

Character-based access to the World Wide Web is very fast as graphic image files don't need to be transferred all the time which can slow things up considerably, and the same information is still available to you. To try out the Web with one of these clients you can Telnet to the birthplace of WWW itself which can be found at:

`info.cern.ch`

When you connect you can explore by following the on-screen prompts and selecting the numbers of the links that interest you. However, to get the best from this type of browser you will need to know a few basic commands. The following guide should be enough for you to browse successfully.

WWW "Line Mode" browser commands

<number>	Follow the hypertext link defined by the specified number
<return key>	Display next page
back	Return to previous document

bottom	Move to bottom of current document
down	Scroll down a page in current document
find <keyword>	Search for specified text, only available when the browser flags that an index is present
go <pathname>	Go to specified document
help	A list of commands and brief descriptions
home	Return to first document read
list	List all links from current document
manual	The on-line manual for the World Wide Web
next	Go to next link in current document
previous	Go to previous link in current document
quit	I bet you can't guess!
recall	List all documents visited so far. Specify a number as an argument to select a specific document from the history list
top	Move to top of current document
up	Scroll up a page in current document
verbose	Toggle "verbose" mode (only really useful if you like lots of code, or are debugging)

As I've already stated, if you want to really see the World Wide Web in its best light then you need to take the graphical route. This isn't the easiest thing in the world, as the client software does take a little bit of setting up, but once you have read the documentation and got going it is

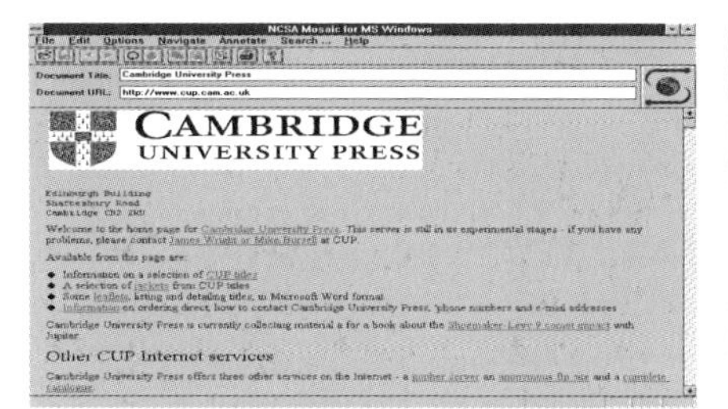

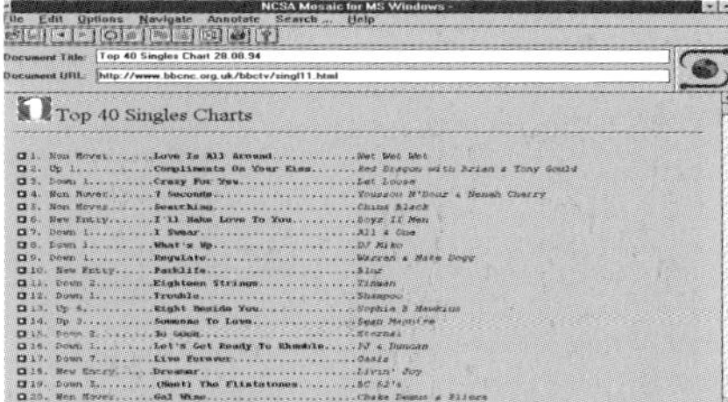

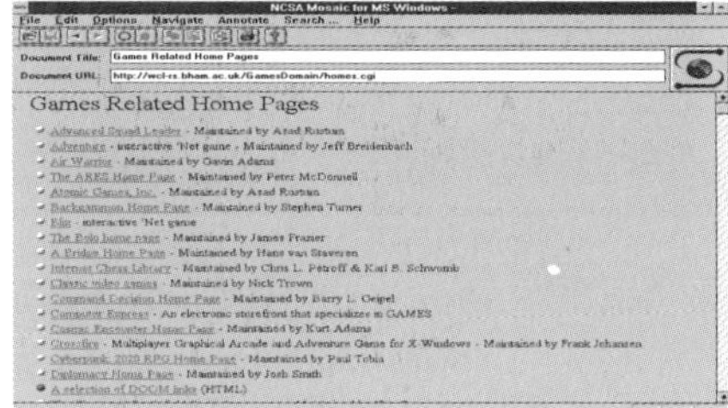

Just a small selection from the wonders of the World Wide Web.

worth every minute you spent on installing it. There isn't enough space here to explore fully either the Web or the Mosaic browser, so you may wish to take a look at the book in this series which is devoted to the World Wide Web and nothing else!

If you are talking about graphical browsers for the Web than at the moment you are really talking about one program, and that is Mosaic. It is still in its testing stages, even though there are millions of people using it world-wide, and versions are available for lots of different platforms including Windows, Amiga, Macintosh, and UNIX. Written and distributed by the National Center for Supercomputing Applications (NCSA) in the US, part of the National Science Foundation, Mosaic has become remarkably popular. I say remarkably for while Mosaic is, without any doubt, an amazing program it is still in Alpha and Beta versions, and

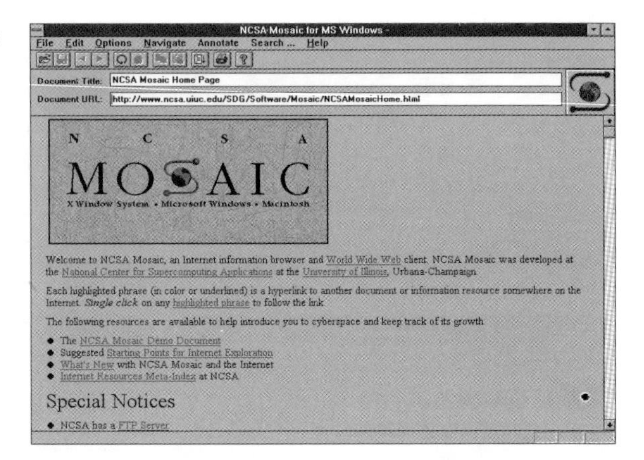

Mosaic above all others has provided an exciting window on the Web.

has a tendency to fall over more often than the horses I back in the Grand National (and that's saying something).

Once you have set up Mosaic it is a pleasure to use, apart from typing in the Uniform Resource Locator (URL) to point the browser at the Web site you want to visit, you will find you won't really need the keyboard. Everything is just point and click; Mosaic automagically decides what type of format the information is and how it should be viewed. So if you have selected a picture, then an image viewer of your choice (which you will have defined when setting up the program) will display it for you.

The only real drawback to all this is that it is all done on-line, while running up someone's telephone bill, and because it is so interesting you can find that you have spent an hour or two exploring without realising it.

Chapter 4
Finding and transferring files

If you think about the sheer volume of files that are stored on the Internet, and we are talking thousands of Gigabytes here, then surely it is the biggest shareware library on the face of the earth. With all that shareware and public domain software out there the chances are you are going to want to download some of it at some stage. Well, don't worry because it really isn't a problem, thanks to FTP and Archie.

FTP is the Internet File Transfer Protocol, and the acronym is also used to describe the actual act of moving files as well, so you see references to files that you can "FTP" from somewhere or other. Archie is a searching tool that will help you find exactly where on the Internet the files that you want are kept.

Don't worry about the security of files on your computer just because you have an Internet account though, people can't log into the Internet and help themselves to your files. By the same token, you can't connect to any computer on the Internet willy nilly and help yourself either. Many FTP sites are only open to those users who have access rights,

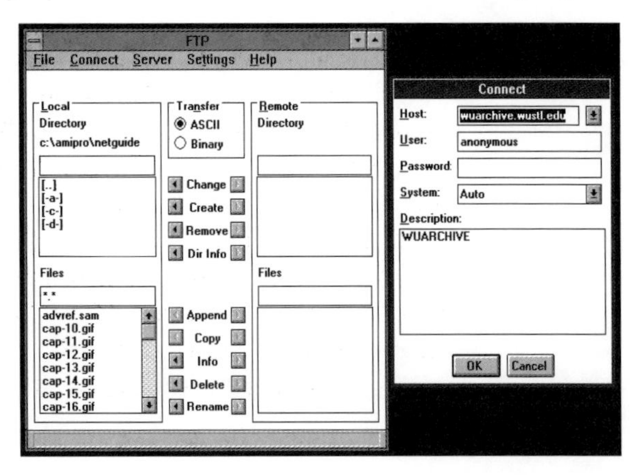

File Transfer Protocol, sounds really boring but it's totally irreplaceable.

this may be through a business or university connection, or you may pay to use a commercial service.

There are, however, hundreds of sites which will let any user in to browse and download files, and these are known as Anonymous FTP Sites. Generally, these sites have a public directory which anyone can access while retaining sensible security restrictions on the rest of their directories. When prompted for a username and password on Anonymous FTP sites, you simply enter "anonymous" and your full email address respectively.

To save time when connecting to an anonymous FTP site you don't have to send your full email address as a password. Instead you can just send `<username>@`, where `<username>` is your account name. For example, instead of typing `dwindera@cix.compulink.co.uk` I would just enter `dwindera@`. This is because the FTP site will already know where you are connecting from, and so only really needs to know who it is who is paying a visit.

The wonderful thing about the Internet is that it really doesn't matter what computer platform you are using, the File Transfer Protocol takes care of the business of sorting out how to move a file from a UNIX-based site to the PC on your desktop, or the Amiga, the Macintosh, or Atari. What matters more is the type of Internet account you have, because this can effect the way in which the transfer will be handled. If you are using a dial-up or terminal connection, the type offered by commercial on-line services such as Cix, Delphi, and the PC User Group, then the file will take twice as long to be downloaded than if you were connecting with a dial-in or SLIP/PPP account.

The reason is simple. With a SLIP/PPP type account you have a direct connection to the Internet so any files you FTP are copied directly from the host site to your computer. If you use a dial-up service then it is they, and not you, who has the direct Internet connection. So when a file is copied it is first transferred to their computer, from where it has to be downloaded to yours. Some services, like Delphi, make this double headed transfer invisible to their users, others ask you to download the FTP'd file from your Internet directory on their system, like Cix. Whichever one you use though, the file is still to be downloaded twice in effect.

Connecting to an Anonymous FTP site is easy enough, providing you know the site name. To find this information you need look no further than the packed to bursting Internet Resource Directory at the end of this book. Select a site that interests you and then follow my lead and connect to the shareware treasure trove of your choice...

Assuming you are already at the internet prompt of your service provider, you would just type

```
ftp <sitename>
```

So if you wanted to connect to the FTP site at ftp.demon.co.uk, which holds a large number of Internet tools and applications, you would enter

```
ftp ftp.demon.co.uk
```

Note that in this example, like many others, it has the name ftp as part of the site. You still need to type this part to be able to connect, typing ftp demon.co.uk in our previous example would not have worked.

When connected, using FTP is fairly straightforward once you have mastered a few important commands. Basically, FTP sites are tree-like structures, comprising directories and sub-directories which contain files. To move around the directory structure, and thus find the files you want to transfer, you need to learn a handful of basic UNIX commands. FTP sites, like most things Internet, tend to run under a UNIX operating system and the following commands will help you navigate successfully:

ascii	set transfer mode to ascii
binary	set transfer mode to binary
cd	move to specified directory
cdup	move back to previous directory
dir	list contents of a directory
get	download a file
help	get a list of commands
mget	download more than one file
put	upload a file
pwd	print the name of the current working directory
quit	exit the FTP session

Most Anonymous FTP sites keep the files that are available for public download in a directory called "pub". Head straight for this directory and you shouldn't go far wrong, take it from Wavey.

You will notice that a lot of the files that are stored at Anonymous FTP sites have strange filename extensions, this is because the files may come from many different computer platforms and so could be archived with all sorts of programs. It is important that you know what these extensions mean, otherwise the files could turn out to be a wasted download. Here is a brief explanation of what archiving programs are denoted by what extension:

Extension	**Archiver**
.arc	pkpak
.arj	arj
.gz	gzip
.hqx	binhex 4.0
.lha	lha
.lzh	lha
.pak	Pak
.pit	Packit
.Sit	Stuffit
.tar	tar
.tar.Z	tar and compress
.zip	pkzip
.zoo	zoo
.z	pack
.Z	compress

Unfortunately, it is a fact of life that there are a number of demented cretins whose idea of pleasure is the writing and spreading of computer viruses. The Internet is an obvious attraction to these people, as it provides the chance to spread their filth to more than 30 million users, all over the world, instantly and easily.

Because of this you should ALWAYS scan any file that you have downloaded from the Internet, or indeed any on-line system, for viruses before you use it. Remember a virus cannot, as far as I am aware, activate until you execute the program. Check it first and if in doubt, throw it out.

There are plenty of very good virus scanners, for all types of operating system, available from Internet FTP sites. Don't worry, you will find that most of these have a method of remaining virus free themselves. Ask around and find out which is the recommended virus checker for your computing platform.

Please don't get too alarmed by this warning though, he says, putting on his best TV crimebuster voice, as viruses are a pretty rare occurrence. It is, you will agree, much better to be safe than sorry though.

It is even possible to transfer files without connecting directly to a FTP site, and this is accomplished with the help

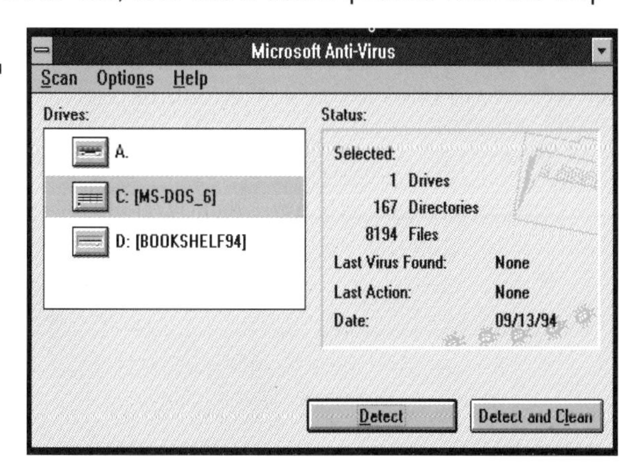

Virus scanners come in many guises, make sure you use one!

of email of all things. FTPMail involves sending an email request for a file to a special server, giving the precise details of what the file is and where it is located, and then the file gets sent to you as a specially encoded email message. The file is converted to text using the UUencode program, so you will need a UUdecode program to unravel it, and if it is large it will be broken down into a number of such messages before being sent to you.

You need to know the exact details of what a file is called and the directory structure where it is stored, so it's likely that you would first need to make a search using Archie (which can also be done using email) to get these details.

All of this means that using FTPMail is a pretty time consuming process, and only really recommended if you have no alternative (which seeing as you have an Internet account you do!).

There is a FTPMail server at **ftpmail@src.doc.ic.ac.uk**, and if you send an email message to this address with no subject line and the single word "help" in the text

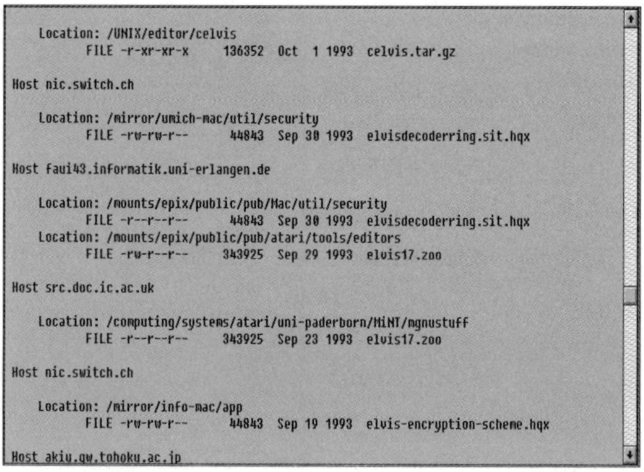

```
    Location: /UNIX/editor/celvis
           FILE -r-xr-xr-x     136352  Oct  1 1993  celvis.tar.gz

Host nic.switch.ch

    Location: /mirror/umich-mac/util/security
           FILE -rw-rw-r--      44843  Sep 30 1993  elvisdecoderring.sit.hqx

Host faui43.informatik.uni-erlangen.de

    Location: /mounts/epix/public/pub/Mac/util/security
           FILE -r--r--r--      44843  Sep 30 1993  elvisdecoderring.sit.hqx
    Location: /mounts/epix/public/pub/atari/tools/editors
           FILE -rw-r--r--     343925  Sep 29 1993  elvis17.zoo

Host src.doc.ic.ac.uk

    Location: /computing/systems/atari/uni-paderborn/MiNT/mgnustuff
           FILE -r--r--r--     343925  Sep 23 1993  elvis17.zoo

Host nic.switch.ch

    Location: /mirror/info-mac/app
           FILE -rw-rw-r--      44843  Sep 19 1993  elvis-encryption-scheme.hqx

Host akiu.gw.tohoku.ac.jp
```

The amazing Archie in action, here is a small part of a report from a search for files containing the word Elvis.

you should receive back full instructions on how to use the service.

Finding files with Archie

I briefly mentioned Archie at the start of this chapter, and now your appetite has been well and truly whetted by all this talk of unlimited free software I dare say you'd like to know a bit more about file finding. Archie, which is derived from the word "archive", was developed at the McGill School of Computer Science in Canada.

You can use this wonderful program to search a database that contains details of all the files held at more than 1,000 Anonymous FTP sites, and that's one heck of a lot of files. Archie will present you with a list of the exact locations of the specified file, right down to the directory path and filename. It is fairly easy to use, but there are different ways of going about it.

- You can use an Archie client already installed by your service provider. Ask them if there is one, or just type "archie" and see what happens!
- You can Telnet to an Archie server, a popular site in the UK is archie.doc.ic.ac.uk where you should use "archie" as a login name.
- You can search the Archie database from within a Gopher, and this is probably the easiest option of them all.
- Finally, you can also use Archie by email, sending a message to **archie@doc.ic.ac.uk** leaving the subject line blank, but including **prog <filename>** in the message text.

Before you start to use Archie you should, to be honest, give some thought to the type of search that you want to perform. There is a choice of four different search types you can choose from:

exact Requires the exact filename of the file you are looking for

regex Archie will treat some of the characters typed in the search string as wildcards, according to UNIX regular expressions. If you don't know what this means, then don't use it

sub A non-case sensitive search for filenames containing or matching the specified string

subcase A case sensitive version of sub

I would recommend that you stick to using the sub search category whenever possible, it's the easiest method of acceptable results.

Once connected to Archie there are a variety of command options open to you, some of the more useful or common ones include:

bugs Displays a list of all currently known bugs in the Archie system

help Lists all valid commands, don't be afraid to use it

list Reports all Internet sites stored in the Archie database, including the last date that the information on each site was updated

mail Use this command to send the output of the last command to a specified email

	address. Useful for emailing the results of file searches to yourself
prog	Probably the most important of the commands, prog is the little beauty that initiates the Archie database search for the specified filename
set	Use this command to set parameters for use during the Archie session
set mailto	Set a default mail address, allowing the mail command to be used without further arguments
set maxhits	Restricts the number of matches made in any Archie search, the default is 1,000 "hits"
set pager	Turn on screen paging
set search	Defines what type of search Archie should perform, choose from exact, regex, sub, and subcase
set sortby	Sets the order in which the output of an Archie search is listed, choose from none, filename, hostname, size, and time
set term	Define the terminal type that you are using
servers	This returns a list of all current Archie servers
show	Display the value of a given variable
site	Lists all the files which are available for FTP from a specified host
unset	Use this if you should ever want to turn off a Boolean variable, which is pretty likely
unset pager	Turn off screen paging

whatis	This command searches a software description database containing names and short descriptions of software resources on the Internet

Archie doesn't accept DOS wildcards, so although you could find a file called "wavey.txt" by searching for both wavey and wavey.txt, just using wav*.txt wouldn't work.

Chapter 5
Using other computers

Telnet is a handy tool that lets you connect to another computer that is part of the Internet and use it as if you were sitting at a keyboard in front of its terminal, even if, in reality, the computer is thousands of miles away. Of course, you can only use Telnet to connect to publicly accessible computers, or computers where you have an account or some other form of access authorisation. Once again, I must reiterate that nobody can just come along and casually connect to your desktop computer and wander freely around your system! You may not see the usefulness of such an application straight away, but perhaps a real example will help to illustrate Telnet's potential.

Say I belong to a commercial on-line system on the opposite side of the planet to where I live. That system has no connection points that are local to me, heck they aren't even in the same country as I am. I couldn't afford to make long distance telephone calls to connect to the system, or justify the cost if I could. However, using Telnet I can first connect to the Internet with my service provider, a local telephone call away, and from there I can Telnet to the on-line system in Japan. I can then use that system exactly as if I had called it directly, but secure in the knowledge that all the time I am using it I am only paying for a local rate telephone call.

Using Telnet is easy enough, you just specify the name of the system you want to connect to. Some Telnet addresses have a number at the end of them, and this is an important part of the address. It is the port number, and refers to the part of that computer network that is publicly accessible. The port number enables you to connect to that specific part of the system, without gaining access anywhere else. Once you have issued your Telnet command you will, if you

Using Telnet to connect to TWICS in Tokyo.

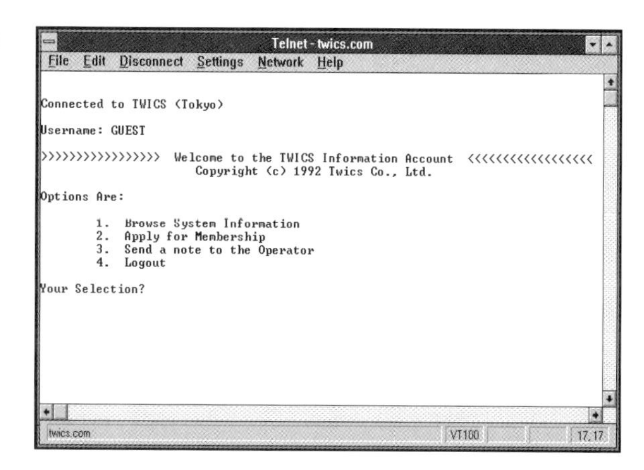

have successfully connected to the remote computer, be asked for your login username and password. Most public sites will ask for a publicly known password and login name, the nicer systems will tell you what these are and prompt your for them. Often all that is required is just your username.

When you have finished your Telnet session you have to log off the remote computer, but this may not always end your Telnet session. To exit cleanly from Telnet type "Ctrl-]". This will place you back at the Telnet prompt from where you can type "Quit" to get back to your Internet prompt.

Sometimes responses can be extremely slow when using Telnet to connect to a busy system. This is due to heavy network traffic and there is nothing you can do about it but try again later.

Chapter 6
Socialising

There are three main ways in which the Internet can be used as a social medium, an arena for making new friends, developing existing friendships, relaxing, or even letting off steam after a hard days work. These are Usenet, Internet Relay Chat, and Mailing Lists. You could call it four ways and add email, but that goes without saying.

Friendships develop quite differently on-line than they do in a real life situation. For a start they tend to build a lot quicker, as there aren't the ordinary barriers caused by physical differences and prejudice. Also, perhaps because there is security in the knowledge that you need never meet the person you are talking to in a face-to-face situation unless you want to, a level of trust and frankness tends to appear much sooner in on-line relationships than in terrestrial ones.

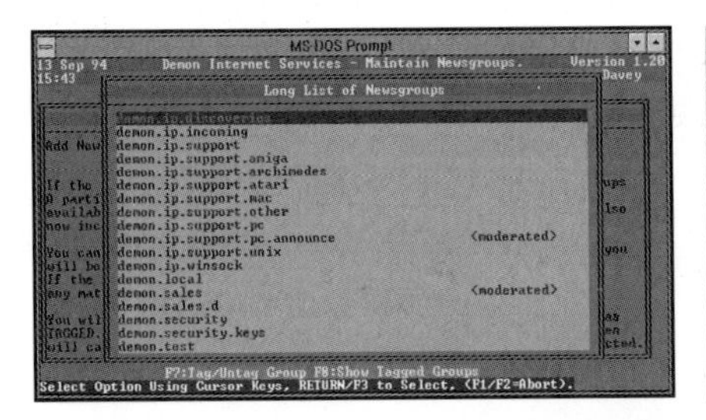

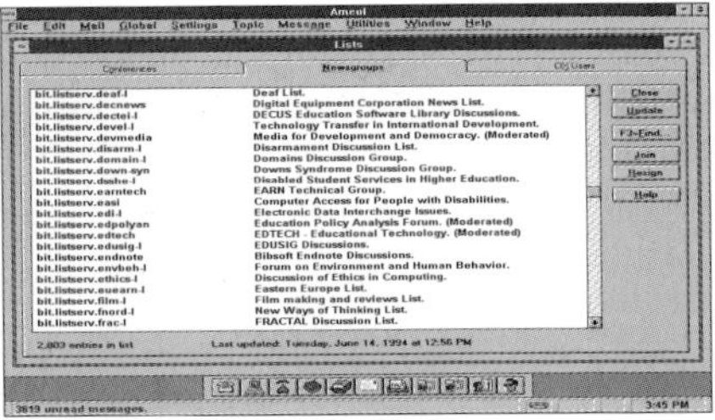

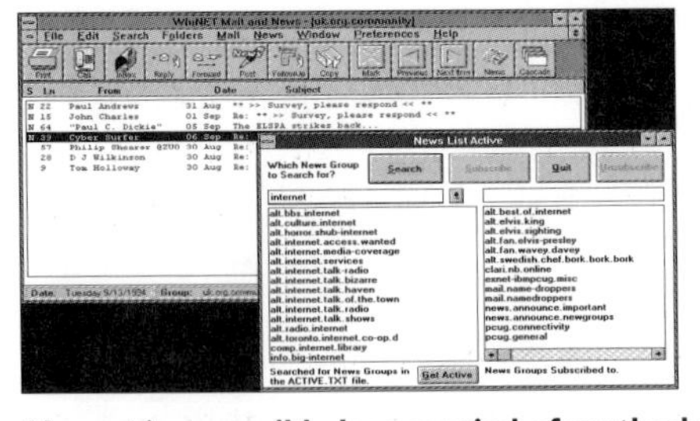

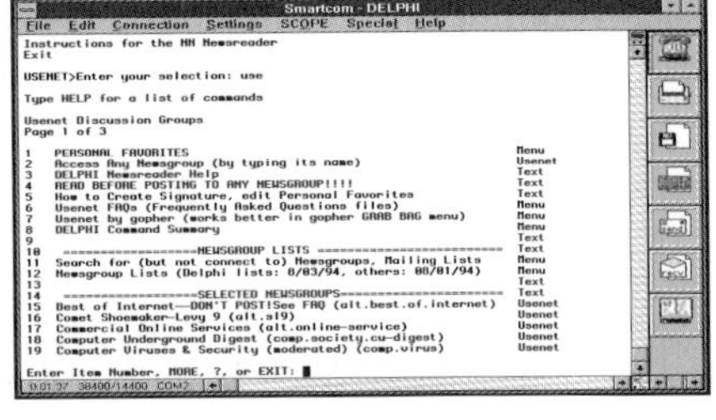

Usenet is accessible by a myriad of methods, choose the one that suits you.

Of course, there has to be a downside to the anonymity factor, and there is. People can be whoever they want to be, maybe the sort of person they could never be in real life, on the Net. This can lead to a kind of dual personality, one for the real world and one for cyberspace. It is not uncommon for someone to pretend to be female in order to attract more "friends" this way. Luckily, the number of truly sad cases on the Internet is greatly outnumbered by the number of ordinary, everyday folk like me (OK that was a bad example).

Usenet

Usenet is used by millions of people on a daily basis, and comprises thousands of "Newsgroups". Each Newsgroup is a forum for discussion on a specific subject matter, if you can think of a subject you would like to talk about I can just about guarantee there is a Usenet Newsgroup out there that exists to accommodate you.

The discussion takes the form of messages, known as articles, which are posted to the Newsgroup by its participants. To participate you need to subscribe to the Newsgroups that interest you. Don't worry, subscription costs nothing but your time and a lot of hard disk space! You also need a special piece of software called a Newsreader, there are lots of these including ones for all popular computing platforms. The chances are that your service provider will have an on-line Newsreader already set up for you to use.

Newsgroups are named to a hierarchy, that is, an ordered structure, so as to distinguish them from each other and help the user to see what the subject matter for discussion is. Each group name comprises a topic and various sub-topics, all the topics are abbreviated for added confusion. So a Newsgroup called comp.lang.c++ is actually shorthand for computer.language.c++

The main topics you will see, remembering that these form only the first section of the Newsgroup name, are:

alt	Alternative newsgroups, covering a wide variety of subject matter. Some of these newsgroups will be rather offensive to many people, and can include subject matter of a very questionable nature
bionet	Newsgroups of interest to Biologists
bit	BITNET listserv mailing list redistribution
biz	For product announcements and so on
clari	A commercial news service, ClariNet
comp	Discussion and information relating to computers
de	German language groups
fj	Japanese language groups
gnu	The Free Software Federation GNU project
hepnet	High Energy Physics researchers group (sounds like an odd type of dance music fanatic to me!)
ieee	The Institute of Electrical and Electronics Engineers.
inet	Another method of distributing high volume groups, the "inet" prefix being used to help

	distinguish from the normally distributed group.
info	University of Illinois mailing list redistribution
k12	Subjects of interest to teachers of children up to the age of 12
misc	Everything that doesn't fit anywhere
elsenews	Discussion and announcements about Usenet
rec	Recreational matters, hobbies etc
relcom	Russian language groups
sci	Newsgroups that discuss the sciences
soc	Social matters, psychology, sociology etc
talk	Chatter and debate, sometimes very strange indeed
u3b	AT&T 3B computer users (it's OK, I'm as confused as the rest of you)
vmsnet	For all DEC VAX/VMS users out there

An important aspect of Usenet is the established code of conduct that exists. This etiquette is commonly know as "Netiquette" and if you break the rules you are likely to get flamed for it. Flaming is the sending of abusive email, or sometimes a posting in a public area, and is the equivalent of a real world rant and rave. To avoid having to wear fire proof underwear, follow this brief guide to Netiquette:

- Always read the Frequently Asked Questions (FAQ) file if there is one
- Don't cross post to lots of Newsgroups

- Use smileys, but don't overdo it
- Don't quote messages excessively
- Don't use an enormous rambling signature
- Keep on topic, don't talk about sheep in the kite flyers group
- Don't use upper case letters all the time, AS THIS IS SHOUTING

You can get a full list of Usenet groups using whichever Newsreader you have available. A lack of space prevents me from including a list in this book, but the Communicating On-line title in this series will feature a large and useful Usenet Directory.

Internet relay chat

IRC is basically like CB Radio, but on the Internet. You can talk to any number of people by joining various "channels" of discussion. The chat is in real time so you can work out expensive it is if you get captivated by the conversation. Although generally regarded as something of a waste of time by most "serious" Internet users, IRC has had its moments. For example, during the Gulf War hundreds of users got together on a single IRC channel to listen to reports of the bombings from users logging in from Iraq. During the Russian coup against Yeltsin in 1993 IRC users in Moscow gave live reports to people all over the world.

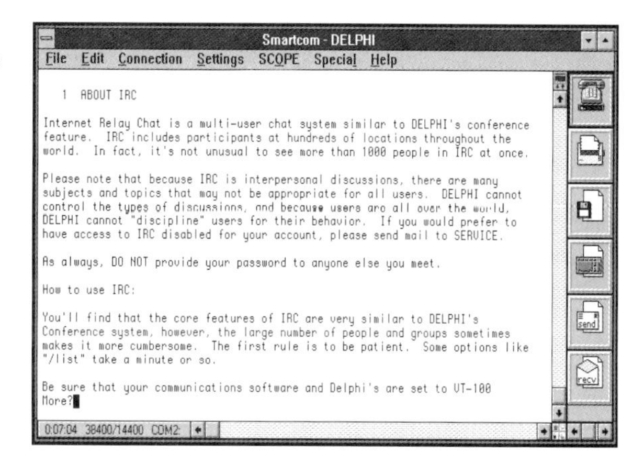

Internet Relay Chat looks pretty boring in a book, it's a different story when you actually start using it though.

Many service providers have IRC clients that you can use, if yours doesn't you will find it hard to get connected any other way. Vast numbers of IRC servers have closed down over the past few months, and it is hard to find places to Telnet to that will accept anonymous users. I did find two public IRC servers that were still running when this book was written, although I can give no guarantees they will still be open for business when you read this:

telnet://sci.dixie.edu 6677

telnet://vinson.ecn.uoknor.edu 6677

Mailing lists

Mailing lists are, essentially, much the same as Usenet Newsgroups in as far as they bring people together to discuss issues in specific interest groups. However, unlike Usenet, all you need to be able to participate in a mailing list is an Internet email address. There are thousands of mailing lists, they cover all sorts of subjects, including many

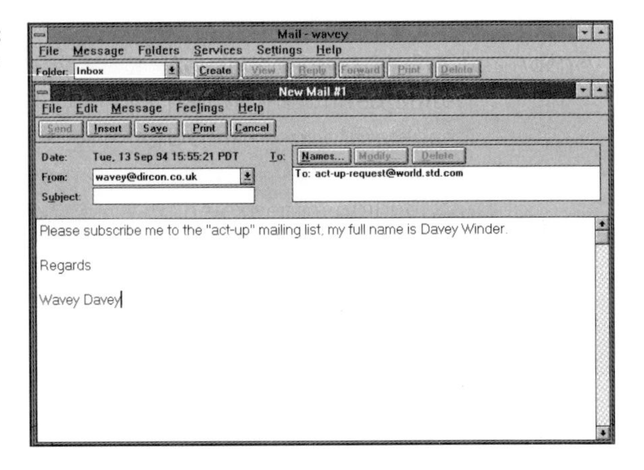

Subscribing to a mailing list is easy, just be prepared for a bulging mailbox.

of the Usenet Newsgroups which are archived and then distributed by this method. Some of the lists are also very busy, the amount of traffic can certainly keep your mailbox full to bursting and will take over your hard disk unless you employ regular pruning procedures.

There are two types of mailing list: ones that are maintained by a real, live, human type organism; and those that are untouched by the human hand and rely on computer programs instead. Generally, you can tell which have the human touch as the address where you have to send your request to be put on the lists distribution will be the list name followed by -request. So a mailing list that goes by the name of 90210 (yes, that TV programme that I don't watch at all) has a subscription address of `90210-request@ferkel.ucsb.edu`, all email sent to this address doesn't appear in the distributed list.

A request for subscription to a list maintained the human way should contain a brief message which includes the mailing list name and your full name.

The most popular computer program that maintains lists is called listserv, and you usually find a host of different mailing lists at any listserv address. To subscribe to one of these you would send a message to the listserv address containing the following text:

```
sub <list> <your name>
```

To unsubscribe from a listserv maintained mailing list you send a message containing the text of:

```
signoff <list>
```

You may also come across other mailing list distribution methods, all of them work in much the same way, but you will need to follow whatever instructions are given to ensure you are doing things correctly. Examples of some of these alternative distribution methods include: Majordomo, Almanac, Mailbase, and Mailserv.

I have not included comprehensive details of mailing lists in the "Internet Resource Directory" for reasons of space, but a large and useful list is contained in the "Communicating On-line" title in this series of books.

If you want to find out what all the listserv mailing lists are, and there are more than 4,000 of them, then you can get this information by sending an email message to:
`listserv@bitnic.educom.edu`
With a body text of:
`list global`

Chapter 7
Reference section

CommUnity is the Computer Communicators' Association, and came into being in the final weeks of 1992. There had been a threat to the survival of Bulletin Board Systems from the combined forces of FAST (the Federation Against Software Theft) and ELSPA (the European Leisure Software Publishers Association). In an effort to try and reduce software theft and piracy, which these organisations perceived was rife on BBSs, they were looking at the possibility of getting legislation to enforce the licensing of Bulletin Boards and On-Line Systems.

The on-line community soon got to hear about these plans, helped along the way by an article I wrote on the subject for *Amiga Shopper* magazine, and decided that it needed a concerted effort to ensure that such legislation should not be allowed to threaten the existence of BBSs (many of which are run on small budgets, without charging their members, and which would have to close if the members were forced to pay a hefty license fee every year).

The result of this was a meeting in London where representatives of all the main networks were present. A

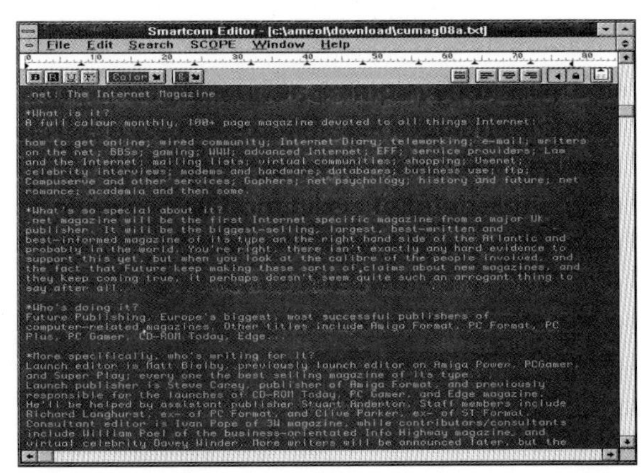

***CommUnicate* is the journal of the Computer Communicators' Association, and is distributed electronically, of course. Here is a recent extract concerning *.net* (The Internet Magazine).**

committee was elected to investigate what could be done, and how to do it, and I was proud to be elected to serve as part of the steering group. It was from these seeds that CommUnity, The Computer Communicators' Association was born. Fortunately, the proposed legislation got nowhere, and following a meeting with FAST, ELSPA, an MP, and members of the on-line community the plans were dropped. CommUnity, however, has continued to grow from strength to strength, and is the UK's leading organisation of, and for, users of on-line systems and networks. With a regular electronic journal called *CommUnicator* and a presence on many BBSs as well as the Internet, I am certain that it will continue to grow.

The aims of the Computer Communicators' Association are:

- To maintain and connect a membership which shares a common concern that access to technology, information, and communication should be as freely available as possible.

- To raise public awareness about issues and opportunities arising from ongoing rapid advances in computer-based communications media.

- To monitor and inform the press and media of computer-based communications, responding to misinformation or prejudice with a coherent voice.

- To develop among policy makers a better understanding of the issues underlying free and open telecommunications, and support legal and structural approaches which ease the assimilation of new technologies by society, and maintain open access to them.

- To support litigation in the public interest to preserve, protect, and extend civil rights within the realm of computing and telecommunications technology.
- To work with agencies and individuals who share our interest in the development of computer-based communications.
- To extend our membership and organisation to include wider Europe, or assist there in the establishment and networking of independent groups sharing our aims.
- To encourage and support educational activities and initiatives which increase popular understanding of the opportunities and challenges posed by developments in computing and telecommunications.
- To encourage and support the development of new tools which ease access to computer-based telecommunications.

The CommUnity constitution also leaves us in no doubt as to what the Computer Communicators' Association isn't, stating that it:

"...shall not seek to control or enforce specific conduct in computer communications users, on-line systems or networks. Shall not enter into any relationship with any other group wherein it becomes required, encouraged or obliged to actively monitor on-line systems, networks or activities for any person. Shall not act as intermediary between complainants or informants and other groups or agencies for the purpose of passing on allegations of, information on, or evidence of, activities by computer communications users, on-line services or networks."

To find out more about CommUnity you can send email to **community@arkham.demon.co.uk** or join the Usenet Newsgroup uk.org.community

Files relating to CommUnity are available by FTP from:

ftp.demon.co.uk/pub/archives/community

The Computer Communicators' Association was originally set up as a voluntary organisation, but funds are always needed to cover the basic administrative costs and to help with lobbying. So to do your bit in ensuring that your rights as an on-line user are protected, why not join CommUnity by sending a cheque for £10 (£5 if unemployed or a student) made payable to "CommUnity" amd semt to the following address:

CommUnity
89 Mayfair Avenue
Worcester Park
Surrey KT4 7SJ

Enclose a short, signed letter requesting membership which must include the following details:

Full name, postal address, email address, and any other information you think may be useful along with your permission to store these details in the CommUnity membership database.

UNIX

Because a large percentage of the Internet uses UNIX-based operating systems, it stands to reason you are going to come across it every now and again. Even though many Internet "Client" programs hide the UNIX side of things from the user, there are times when you will be best served if you have a knowledge of the basic commands.

With this in mind I have prepared what is possibly the most concise guide to UNIX in the history of the Operating System! I'm not even going to pretend that it is comprehensive, as it plainly isn't. What it is, I hope, is enough to let you get out of trouble while using the Internet, should the need arise.

UNIX command reference

>	Directs the output to a file
>>	Appends to a file
<	Directs input from a file
Ctrl/C	Interrupt current process
Ctrl/D	Exit, log out
Ctrl/H	Backspace
Ctrl/J	Terminal reset
Ctrl/S	Stop display scrolling
Ctrl/U	Clear command line
Ctrl/Q	Restart display scrolling
cat	Display file on screen
cd	Change to home directory
cd	Change to specified directory
cdup	Change to previous directory
cp	Copy

grep	Search for text in file
head	Display first few lines of a file
ls	Lists contents of current directory
ls] more	Lists contents of current directory but with the More prompt
mkdir	Create directory
mv	Move
passwd	Change your password
pwd	Prints full pathname of current directory
r	Repeat command
rm	Remove file
rmdir	Remove empty directory
tail	Display last few lines of a file
whoami	Display username

Smiley dictionary

Because it can be difficult to express emotional content within a plain text message, and very easy to interpret a message the wrong way, a system of smileys (or emote-icons for any of our American friends reading this) has been developed and is now in widespread use. A smiley is a small face made of standard characters, look at them sideways on if you still haven't fallen in, and can help convey feelings ranging from sad to mad to glad. Also there are now smileys to cover much more than just these standard emotions, and as you can see from this dictionary they are not all to be taken too seriously.

Smiley	Meaning
:-||	Angry
(:-)	Bald
:-)	Basic happy

:-(Basic sad
B-) Batman
:-)> Bearded
%+(Beaten up
?-) Black eye
:-)X Bow tie
R-) Broken glasses
:^) Broken nose
|:-) Bushy eyebrows
) Cheshire cat
<|-) Chinese
3:-) Cow
:-t Cross
X-) Cross eyed
:’-(Crying
i-) Detective (private eye)
:-e Disappointed
:-)’ Drooling
{:V Duck
<:-) Dumb question
5:-) Elvis
>:-) Evil grin
:’’’-(Floods of tears
:-! Foot in mouth
/:-) French
8) Frog
::-) Glasses wearer (1)
8-) Glasses wearer (2)
8:) Gorilla
:-’) Has a cold (1)
:*) Has a cold (2)
:-| Hmmmph!
:-C Jaw hits floor
.-) Keeping an eye out

:-#	Kiss (1)
:-*	Kiss (2)
:-X	Kiss (3)
:+)	Large nose
:-D	Laughing out loud
:-}	Leering
(-:	Left handed
:-9	Licking lips
:-}	Lipstick wearer
:- |	Monkey
:-{	Moustache (1)
:-#)	Moustache (2)
(-)	Needs haircut
:^)	Nose out of joint
:8)	Pig
:-?	Pipe smoker
=:-)	Punk
:-"	Pursed lips
|-]	Robocop
O:-)	Saint
:-@	Screaming
:-O	Shocked
:-V	Shouting
|-)	Sleeping
:-i	Smoker (1)
:-Q	Smoker (2)
:-j	Smoker smiling
:-6	Sour taste in mouth
:-v	Speaking
:-w	Speaks with forked tongue
*-)	Stoned
:-T	Tight lipped
:-p	Tongue in cheek
:-&	Tongue tied

:-/ Undecided
:-[Vampire (1)
:-|< Vampire (2)
:-< Vampire (3)
:-)= Vampire (4)
:-)) Very happy
:-((Very sad
:-c Very unhappy
C|:-) Wearing bowler hat
d:-) Wearing cap
[:-) Wearing headphones
:-(#) Wears teeth braces
;-) Winking
:-7 Wry smile
|-O Yawning

Acronym dictionary

Because time equals money, and never more so than in the world of on-line communications, people have devised ways of saving typing time by reducing common phrases into acronyms. These are known as TLAs, or Three Letter Acronyms, although many are not truly acronyms and few actually have three letters. Oh well, such is life. There are a whole lorry-load of these TLAs around, and I dare say I have missed some, but I hope this dictionary will cover the ones that are in most common usage and should go a long way to help you make sense of some seemingly senseless terms.

Acronym	Meaning
AFAICT	As Far As I Can Tell
AFAIK	As Far As I Know
AFK	Away From Keyboard

AIUI	As I Understand It
B4	Before
BAK	Back At Keyboard
BBL	Be Back Later
BCNU	Be seeing you
BRB	Be Right Back
BSF	But Seriously Folks
BST	But Seriously Though
BTDT	Been There Done That
BTSOOM	Beats The Shit Out Of Me
BTW	By The Way
BWQ	Buzz Word Quotient
CLM	Career Limiting Move
CUL	See you later
DWIM	Do What I Mean
DWISNWID	Do What I Say Not What I Do
DYJHIW	Don't You Just Hate It When...
ESAD	Eat Shit And Die
ETLA	Extended Three Letter Acronym
EOF	End Of File
F2F	Face-to-Face
FAQ	Frequently Asked Question
FFS	For Fucks Sake
FOAD	Fuck Off And Die
FOAF	Friend Of A Friend
FOC	Free Of Charge
FUBAR	Fucked Up Beyond All Recognition
FWIW	For What It's Worth
FYA	For Your Amusement
FYE	For Your Entertainment
FYI	For Your Information
<G>	Grin
GA	Go Ahead
GAL	Get A Life

GIGO	Garbage In Garbage Out
GR&D	Grinning Running & Ducking
HHOJ	Ha Ha, Only Joking
HHOS	Ha Ha, Only Serious
IAE	In Any Event
IANAL	I Am Not A Lawyer
IBN	I'm Buck Naked
IIRC	If I Recall Correctly
IMBO	In My Bloody Opinion
IME	In My Experience
IMHO	In My Humble Opinion
IMNSHO	In My Not So Humble Opinion
IMO	In My Opinion
IOW	In Other Words
IRL	In Real Life
ISTM	It Seems To Me
ISTR	I Seem To Recall
ITRO	In The Region Of
ITRW	In The Real World
IWBNI	It Would Be Nice If
IYSWIM	If You See What I Mean
JAM	Just A Minute
KISS	Keep It Simple, Stupid
L8R	Later
LOL	Laughs Out Loud
MFTL	My Favourite Toy Language
MORF	Male Or Female?
MOTAS	Member Of The Appropriate Sex
MOTOS	Member Of The Opposite Sex
MOTSS	Member Of The Same Sex
MUD	Multi User Dungeon
MUG	Multi User Game
NALOPKT	Not A Lot Of People Know That
NFWM	No Fucking Way Man!

NIFOC	Nude In Front Of Computer
NRN	No Reply Necessary
OAO	Over And Out
OBTW	Oh, By The Way
OEM	Original Equipment Manufacturer
OIC	Oh, I See
OMG	Oh My God
OTOH	On The Other Hand
OTT	Over The Top
PD	Public Domain
PITA	Pain In The Arse
POD	Piece Of Data
RFD	Request For Discussion
ROFL	Rolls On Floor Laughing
RSN	Real Soon Now
RTFAQ	Read The FAQ
RTFM	Read The Fucking Manual
RUOK	Are you OK
SITD	Still In The Dark
SMOP	Small Matter Of Programming
SNAFU	Situation Normal, All Fucked Up
SNR	Signal to Noise Ratio
SO	Significant Other
SOL	Shit Outta Luck
STFU	Shut The Fuck Up
TANSTAAFL	There Ain't No Such Thing As A Free Lunch
TCB	Trouble Came Back
TDM	Too Damn Many
TIA	Thanks In Advance
TIC	Tongue In Cheek
TLA	Three Letter Acronym
TNX	Thanks
TPTB	The Powers That Be
TTFN	Ta Ta For Now

TTYL	Talk To You Later
TVM	Thanks Very Much
UBD	User Brain Damage
VC	Virtual Community
VR	Virtual Reality
WIBNI	Would It Be Nice If
WRT	With Regard To
WTF	What The Fuck
WTH	What The Hell
WYSIWYG	What You See Is What You Get
YABA	Yet Another Bloody Acronym
YHBM	You Have Bin Mail
YHM	You Have Mail

Chapter 8
Internet resource directory

I have adopted the use of URLs in the resource directories within this book. A URL is a Uniform Resource Locator, and is fast becoming the standard way of addressing Internet resources. URLs are easy to understand, but here's my quick explanation of how to use them anyway.

A URL is comprised of two parts, the actual resource address and a descriptor to identify the particular Internet resource in question. These two parts are separated by a "://" and everything before this separator is the resource descriptor, everything after it, the address.

A descriptor may be Telnet, http (which refers to World Wide Web), ftp, gopher, or mailto (for mailing lists and email). For example, if I was pointing you towards a directory called pub held at the **ftp.demon.co.uk** site, the URL would be:

ftp://**ftp.demon.co.uk/pub**

Remember, it is only the part after the :// separator that you need to type, everything before this is just the description of the Internet resource concerned.

Subject: **3W MAGAZINE**
Description: The WWW pages for Ivan Pope's 3W Magazine which covers all aspects of the Internet
URL: http://**www.3W.com/3W/**

Subject: **ACRONYMS ON-LINE**
Description: An on-line acronym dictionary for all those obscure computer terms
URL: gopher://**info.mcc.ac.uk**

Subject: **ACT-UP**
Description: The Act-Up AIDS awareness mailing list, looking at the work of the various Act-Up groups world-wide which discuss the poltics of AIDS and AIDS related health care
URL: mailto://**act-up-request@world.std.com**

Subject: **AIDS (1)**
Description: Information about Acquired Immune Deficiency Syndrome
URL: gopher://**selway.umt.edu 700**

Subject: **AIDS (2)**
Description: AIDS related mailing list
URL: mailto://**aids-request@cs.ucla.edu**

Subject: **ALLERGIES**
Description: The National Institute for Allergy and Infectious Disease
URL: gopher://**gopher.niaid.nih.gov/1**

Subject: **ANCIENT HISTORY**
Description: The Princeton University Library archives. To connect press "Return Key" and when you see the "#" sign, type call 500
URL: telnet://**pucable.princeton.edu**

Subject: **ANTARCTICA**
Description: The International Centre for Antarctic Information and Research, New Zealand
URL: http://**icair.iac.org.nz/**

Subject: **ARCHAEOLOGY (1)**
Description: The National Archaeological Database contains more than 100,000 reports of archaeological investigations, which can be searched using various criteria. Use the login of **nadb**
URL: telnet://**cast.uark.edu**

Subject: **ARCHAEOLOGY (2)**
Description: The Department of Classical Studies, at the University of Michigan
URL: http://**rome.classics.lsa.umich.edu/welcome.html**

Subject: **ASCII ART**
Description: A collection of the best and worst in ASCII art, that is pictures that are drawn completely using text characters
URL: gopher://**pfsparc02.phil15.uni-sb.de**

Subject: **AUSTRALIAN ART**
Description: A collection of Australian art from both the Australian National Gallery and the Australian National University
URL: http://**www.ncsa.uiuc.edu/SDG/Experimental/anu-art-history/home.html**
or http://**rubens.anu.edu.au/**

Subject: **AYURVEDA**
Description: Ayurveda is the ancient science of life, and this is the mailing list
URL: mailto://**ayurveda-request@netcom.com**

Subject: **BAGPIPES**
Description: Boy are you glad I'm here, because I just know you were hoping I'd tell you where you can find files relating to bagpipes. Weren't you?
URL: ftp://**cs.dartmouth.edu**

Subject: **BALLROOM DANCING**
Description: The mailing list for the ballroom dancing enthusiast. I have a pair of ballroom trousers, but that's another story altogether
URL: mailto://**ballroom-request@athena.mit.edu**

Subject: **BBC**
Description: The BBC Networking Club, TV listings, talk to BBC producers, feedback on programmes, and a heck of a lot more
URL: http://**www.bbcnc.org.uk**

Subject: **BEER (1)**
Description: All you ever needed to know about beer, and lots you didn't
URL: http://**guraldi.itn.med.umich.edu/Beer**

Subject: **BEER (2)**
Description: Recipes for brewing ones own bevy
URL: ftp://**ftp.spies.com/Library/Untech/alcohol.mak**

Subject: **BLINDNESS**
Description: The Blind News Digest mailing list
URL: mailto://**listserv@vm1.nodak.edu**

Subject: **BONSAI TREES**
Description: If you like small ones, trees that is, then this mailing list is for you
URL: mailto://**listserv@cms.cc.wayne.edu**

Subject: **BRITISH CONSTITUTIONAL LAW**
Description: The University of Texas law library archives, use the login of **Library**
URL: telnet://**tallons.law.utexas.edu**

Subject: **BUDDHISM**
Description: Lots of information about the Buddhist religion
URL: ftp://**coombs.anu.edu/coombspapers/otherarchives**

Subject: **BIBLE**
Description: This is the King James version, which probably means more to you than it does to me
URL: gopher://**joeboy.micro.umn.edu**

Subject: **BOOKSHOP**
Description: The On-Line Bookstore, selling electronic texts, what else?
URL: gopher://**akasha.tic.com**

Subject: **BOTANY**
Description: The Botany Department of the University of Georgia
URL: http://**dogwood.botany.uga.edu/**

Subject: **BRITISH LIBRARY**
Description: The British Library is now on-line with this gopher server that contains information about the library and events held there
URL: gopher://**portico.bl.uk**

Subject: **CAMBRIDGE UNIVERSITY PRESS (1)**
Description: The history of the Cambridge University Press, which dates back to 1534, also extracts from popular titles
URL: http://**www.cup.cam.ac.uk**

Subject: **CAMBRIDGE UNIVERSITY PRESS (2)**
Description: Information for authors, details of publications, etc
URL: gopher://**gopher.cup.cam.ac.uk**

Subject: **CAVING**
Description: The caving enthusiasts mailing list
URL: mailto://**cavers-request@clsi.bu.edu**

Subject: **CHEMISTRY**
Description: The Chemistry Department of the University of Sheffield
URL: http://**mac043025.shef.ac.uk/chemistry/chemistry-home.html**

Subject: **CIA WORLD FACTBOOK**
Description: The US Central Intelligence Agency annual report, which contains a wealth of knowledge about almost 250 nations
URL: gopher://**gopher.micro.umn.edu**

Subject: **COKE MACHINES**
Description: Yep, those on-line Coke machines that you can "finger" have arrived on the World Wide Web
URL: http://**www.cs.cmu.edu:8001/afs/cs.cmu.edu/user/bsy/www/coke.html**

Subject: **COMICS**
Description: A mailing list for collectors and readers of non-mainstream comics
URL: mailto://**comix-request@world.std.com**

Subject: **COMPUTER UNDERGROUND DIGEST**
Description: CUD is the journal of hacking and cyberspace, and a bloody good read as well
URL: ftp://**etext.archive.umich.edu/pub/Zines/CUD**

Subject: **COMMUNITY**
Description: The Computer Communicators' Association. Files relating to CommUnity can be found in this archive, including a membership application form
URL: ftp://**ftp.demon.co.uk/pub/archives/community**

Subject: **COOKERY**
Description: An archive of postings to cookery oriented Usenet Newsgroups, containing lots of scrummy recipes
URL: http://**www.vuw.ac.nz/non-local/recipes-archive/recipe-archive.html**

Subject: **COOKIES**
Description: Not the type that you eat, but those wonderful quotes, sayings, thoughts, and pieces of nonsense that change every day. This is the Internet version, every time you Telnet to the Cookie Server it will show you a different, random, Cookie
URL: telnet://**argo.temple.edu 12345**

Subject: **COOKING**
Description: An archive of recipes
URL: ftp://**gatekeeper.dec.com/pub/recipes**

Subject: **CROWLEY**
Description: The texts of Aleister Crowley, one of the fathers of modern witchcraft
URL: ftp://**slopoke.mlb.semi.harris.com/pub/magick/magick/Crowley**

Subject: **CYBERPUNK**
Description: A host of Cyberpunk related articles
URL: gopher://**wiretap.spies.com**

Subject: **DANCE**
Description: Material of interest to dancers and, indeed, those who like dance
URL: ftp://**ftp.cs.dal.ca/comp.archives/rec.arts.dance**

Subject: **DANCE MUSIC**
Description: Dance music in the UK
URL: http://**www.tecc.co.uk/tqm/uk-dance**

Subject: **DATABASES**
Description: Where to find commercial and free databases on the Internet
URL: gopher://**sunic.sunet.se**

Subject: **DEAD SEA SCROLLS**
Description: The World Wide Web Dead Sea Scrolls Exhibition, an excellent on-line version of the Library of Congress exhibition
URL: http://**sunsite.unc.edu/expo/deadsea.scrolls.exhibit/intro.html**

Subject: **DEAFNESS**
Description: Resources for deaf people, but with a USA bias unfortunately
URL: gopher://**cl.msu.edu**

Subject: **DEMON**
Description: The Demon Internet FTP site where you can find a cornucopia of Internet access tools and documentation
URL: ftp://**ftp.demon.co.uk**

Subject: **DEPECHE MODE**
Description: The Depeche Mode mailing list, if you "Enjoy The Silence" you'll love this
URL: mailto://**bongrequest@lestat.compaq.com**

Subject: **DICTIONARY (ENGLISH)**
Description: You will find a decent English dictionary on-line at the University of Michigan library. When asked which host you want, reply Help
URL: telnet://**cts.merit.edu**

Subject: **DINOSAURS**
Description: The dinosaur lovers mailing list
URL: mailto://**dinosaur-request@ctsx.celtech.com**

Subject: **DISABILITY (1)**
Description: Information about disability related issues
URL: gopher://**val-dor.cc.buffalo.edu**

Subject: **DISABILITY (2)**
Description: You will find something like 40 directories here that cover all types of disability
URL: ftp://**handicap.shel.isc-br.com**

Subject: **DISCOGRAPHIES**
Description: Lots of discographies of lots of groups. That is listings of records released, rather than graphs of people dancing in a silly manner
URL: ftp://**ftp.spies.com/Library/Music/Disc**

Subject: **DISNEY**
Description: Everything Walt Disney is here
URL: ftp://**quartz.rutgers.edu/pub/disney**

Subject: **EDUPAGE**
Description: IT news and views, mainly taken from the Internet itself
URL: http://**www.ee.surrey.ac.uk**

Subject: **EFF**
Description: The Electronic Frontier Foundation has its own gopher
URL: gopher://gopher.eff.org

Subject: **ELECTRONIC NEWS**
Description: The Electronic News Stand provides access to many different electronic journals, newspapers, etc. Login as **news**
URL: telnet://**enews.com**

Subject: **ELVIS**
Description: Elvis is alive and well and living in Cyberspace
URL: http://**tamsun.tamu.edu/~ahb2188/elvishom.html**

Subject: **ERIC**
Description: The Educational Resources Information Centre database. Of interest to teachers, or indeed, anyone interested in educational matters Use the login of **sonia**
URL: telnet://**sklib.usask.ca**

Subject: **ETHERNET**
Description: Information about Local Area Networks using Ethernet, reading list, FAQ and more
URL: http://**wwwhost.ots.utexas.edu/ethernet/ethernet-home.html**

Subject: **EXPEDITION**
Description: A research expedition about the Belize rain cycle
URL: http://**seawifs.gsfc.nasa.gov/JASON/JASON.html**

Subject: **EXPO**
Description: An amazing collection of WWW "exhibitions"
URL: http://**sunsite.unc.edu/expo/ticket_office.html**

Subject: **EYE WEEKLY**
Description: A Toronto arts newspaper, back issues of which are available fromthis gopher
URL: gopher://**gopher.io.org**

Subject: **FANTASY BOOKSTORE**
Description: An on-line bookshop with a science fiction and fantasy bias
URL: http://**www.commerce.digital.com/palo-alto/FutureFantasy/hom e.html**

Subject: **FICTION WRITERS**
Description: The Fiction Writers Group is a forum for both the professional and wannabee fiction writer
URL: mailto://**writers-request@studguppy.lanl.gov**

Subject: **FINANCE**
Description: Stock Market quotes, a free "trailer" service for a commercial concern called QuoteCom
URL: http://**www.quote.com/**

Subject: **FINE ART FORUM**
Description: An on-line magazine for people interested in the arts
URL: http://**www.msstate.edu/Fineart_Online/home.html**

Subject: **FRIENDS AND PARTNERS**
Description: A project aimed at aiding communication between the Russian and American people. Use the login of **friends**
URL: telnet://**solar.rtd.utk.edu**

Subject: **FROGS**
Description: Lots of froggy things!
URL: http://**www.cs.yale.edu/HTML/YALE/CS/HyPlans/loosemore-sandr a/froggy.html**

Subject: **GAMES (1)**
Description: Links to On-line Games
URL: http://**wcl-rs.bham.ac.uk/GamesDomain**

Subject: **GAMES (2)**
Description: This is a must for any fans of on-line gaming. Games available include such classics as Tetris and Nethack. Use the login of **games**
URL: telnet://**castor.tat.physik.uni-tuebingen.de**

Subject: **GAY ISSUES**
Description: GayNet is a mailing list for gays, lesbians, and bisexuals
URL: mailto://**majordomo@queernet.org**

Subject: **GUITAR**
Description: Guitar chords and tablature in downloadable format
URL: ftp://**ftp.nevada.edu/pub/guitar**

Subject: **HISTORY TODAY**
Description: What happened on this day in history?
URL: gopher://**uts.mcc.ac.uk**

Subject: **HORSE RACING**
Description: The mailing list for all horse racing fans
URL: mailto://**derby-request@ekrl.com**

Subject: **HUBBLE SPACE TELESCOPE**
Description: Lots of interesting things from Hubble and the Space Telescope Science Foundation
URL: ftp://**stsci.edu**

Subject: **IMPERIAL COLLEGE (1)**
Description: The Imperial College, Department of Computing, gopher. Lots of interesting things here, just connect and have a look around
URL: gopher://**src.doc.ic.ac.uk**

Subject: **IMPERIAL COLLEGE (2)**
Description: The Department of Computing, Imperial College. The World Wide Web site this time
URL: http://**src.doc.ic.ac.uk**

Subject: **INTERNET FAQ**
Description: If you are want answers to even more FAQ's than you get in this book (what surely not possible?) then try looking here
URL: ftp://**rtfm.mit.edu/pub/usenet/news.answers/internet-services**

Subject: **INTERNET SOCIETY**
Description: Lots of interesting statistics and facts about the Internet can be found at the home of the Internet Society
URL: http://**info.isoc.org**

Subject: **INTERNIC**
Description: InterNIC provides a number of services aimed at helping you to get connected and use the Internet. Also directories of Internet sites and resources. Use the login of **guest**
URL: telnet://**ds.internic.net**

Subject: **JARGON**
Description: A hypertext version of the computing jargon dictionary
URL: http://**web.cnam.fr/bin.html/By_Searchable_Index**

Subject: **JEWISHNET**
Description: The Global Jewish Information Network
URL: http://**www.huji.ac.il/www_jewishn/www/t01.html**

Subject: **JOKES**
Description: A massive jokes database that can be searched against any keyword you care to enter
URL: gopher://**uts.mcc.ac.uk/Gopher Services/The Joke File**

Subject: **JUGGLING**
Description: The juggling information service, no less
URL: http://**www.hal.com/services/juggle**

Subject: **KAMA SUTRA**
Description: The electronic version of this famous classic guide to love making
URL: ftp://**quartz.rutgers.edu/pub/sex/kama.sutra**

Subject: **KIDLINK**
Description: This is a project for children between the ages of 10 and 15 years to encourage them to get involved in comms technology. Adults are not allowed, even big kids like Wavey Davey
URL: gopher://**kids.ccit.duq.edu/KIDLINK Gopher**

Subject: **KING ARTHUR**
Description: Files, pictures and documentation relating to King Arthur and Camelot
URL: ftp://**sapphire.epcc.ed.ac.uk/pub/camelot**

Subject: **KORAN**
Description: The Koran in electronic format. This is the Shakir translation of the holy text
URL: ftp://**quake.think.com/pub/etext/koran**

Subject: **MAILING LISTS**
Description: A list of all the mailing lists there are. This is the big one, it's bigger than a very big thing that's about to explode!
URL: ftp://**ftp.nisc.sri.com/netinfo/interest-groups**

Subject: **MAASTRICHT TREATY**
Description: The text of the Maastricht Treaty
URL: gopher://**wiretap.spies.com**

Subject: **MICROSOFT**
Description: Microsoft's own WWW server
URL: http://**www.microsoft.com**

Subject: **MONTY PYTHON**
Description: Scripts and Screenplays from the Monty Python gang
URL: ftp://**nic.funet.fi/pub/culture/tv+film/series/MontyPython**

Subject: **MOVIE DATABASE (1)**
Description: Search for information on actors and actresses, films, producers. More informed than Barry Norman, or not, as the case may be
URL: http://**www.cm.cf.ac.uk/Movies/moviewquery.html**

Subject: **MOVIE DATABASE (2)**
Description: An on-line film database which you can search for information about movies, producers, actors, scripts. It works really well, I've used it a lot
URL: gopher://**info.mcc.ac.uk/Miscellaneous items/Film Database**

Subject: **MULTIMEDIA**
Description: A treasure trove of multimedia resources
URL: http://**cui_www.unige.ch/OSG/MultimediaInfo/**

Subject: **MUSICALS**
Description: The lyrics to a number of famous musicals including *Les Miserables, Phantom of the Opera, Rocky Horror Picture Show,* and *Eric Makes a Teapot*. I might have made one of those up though...
URL: gopher://**quartz.rutgers.edu**

Subject: **NASA (1)**
Description: How many ears has Mr Spock got? The answer is three, a left ear, a right ear, and a final frontier. Answers to many much more useful astronomical questions can be found at the NASA Extragalactic Database. Use the login of **ned**
URL: telnet://**denver.ipac.caltech.edu**

Subject: **NASA (2)**
Description: The NASA Centre, for all you spacey requirements
URL: http://**mosaic.larc.nasa.gov/NASA_homepage.html**

Subject: **NATURAL HISTORY (1)**
Description: The Natural History Museum (London). A behind the scenes exhibit and links to the museum Gopher and FTP sites
URL: http://**www.nhm.ac.uk**

Subject: **NATURAL HISTORY (2)**
Description: A natural history museum exhibit
URL: http://**ucmpl.berkeley.edu/welcome.html**

Subject: **NETWORK NEWS**
Description: The InterNIC Internet magazine
URL: http://**www.internic.net/newsletter**

Subject: **NEW ZEALAND**
Description: The New Zealand tourist guide
URL: http://**www.cs.cmu.edu:8001/Web/People/mjw/NZ/MainPage.html**

Subject: **NURSING**
Description: Yes, a gopher for nurses and nursing issues
URL: gopher://**crocus.esv.warwick.ac.uk**

Subject: **ORIGAMI**
Description: Instructions on everything from how to make a lovely hat right through to how to spend many a joyous evening folding paper into a life-size replica of Frank Bruno. Well, lots of hints for Origami fans anyway...
URL: ftp://**nstn.ns.ca/listserv/origami-l**

Subject: **OTIS (1)**
Description: The OTIS project is an ambitious on-line picture gallery, with hundreds of pictures, animations, and files of interest to art lovers
URL: ftp://**aql.gatech.edu/pub/OTIS**

Subject: **OTIS (2)**
Description: The OTIS image gallery World Wide Web style
URL: http://**sunsite.unc.edu/otis/otis.html**

Subject: **OXFAM**
Description: The official Oxfam "Hunger Web"
URL: http://**www.hunger.brown.edu/oxfam**

Subject: **OXFORD UNIVERSITY LIBRARY**
Description: Texts from the Oxford University library, a massive resource
URL: gopher://**gopher.lib.ox.ac.uk/00/Info/OLIS**

Subject: **PAGANS**
Description: A mailing list that discusses all aspects of Paganism
URL: mailto://**request@drycas.club.cc.cmu.edu**

Subject: **PEN PALS**
Description: The idea of this mailing list is to get kids together as electronic pen-pals
URL: mailto://**pen-pals-request@mainstream.com**

Subject: **PHOTOGRAPHY**
Description: The Panix Photographic Database containing mainly technical information and advice about photography
URL: gopher://**gopher.panix.com**

Subject: **PGP**
Description: Lots of information about Pretty Good Privacy, the public key encryption utility, can be found here
URL: ftp://**ftp.uu.net**

Subject: **PMC-MOO**
Description: This is the Postmodern Culture MOO, a virtual reality environment where you can talk and interact with various odd people in real time
URL: telnet://**dewey.lib.ncsu.edu**

Subject: **POSTAL CODES**
Description: A list of European postal codes. Happy happy joy joy, your life is now complete...
URL: ftp://**nic.funet.fi/pub/doc/mail/stamps**

Subject: **PRATCHETT**
Description: Loads and loads of files relating to Terry Pratchett and his Discworld novels, nay masterpieces!
URL: ftp://**ftp.cs.pdx.edu/pub/pratchett**

Subject: **PROJECT GUTENBERG**
Description: Classics of literature in electronic format
URL: gopher://**gopher.umn.edu**

Subject: **QUOTATIONS**
Description: The Oxford Dictionary of Familiar Quotations in a searchable on-line format. Once connected you want to go to "library" and then "reference"
URL: telnet://**info.rutgers.edu**

Subject: **RADIO**
Description: The AM/FM On-line UK radio magazine
URL: http:/**/www.tecc.co.uk/tqm/amfm**

Subject: **REN AND STIMPY**
Description: Oh Happy Happy, Joy Joy, Happy Happy, Joy Joy. A haven for all fans of Ren and Stimpy
URL: gopher://**quartz.rutgers.edu/ Television and Movies**

Subject: **RUSSIA**
Description: The Friends and Partners project is a joint effort by people from both Russia and the USA to help communication between the two nations
URL: http://**solar.rtd.utk.edu/friends/ home.html**

Subject: **SOVIET ARCHIVE**
Description: An exhibition of everything Soviet, truly informative and interesting
URL: http://**sunsite.unc.edu/expo/soviet.exhibit/soviet.archive.h tml**

Subject: **SPORT**
Description: A gopher with a large sports section, which has a refreshing UK bias including such things as football and cricket
URL: gopher://**govan.cent.gla.ac.uk**

Subject: **STERLING**
Description: A collection of texts by Bruce Sterling, daddy of Cyberpunk
URL: gopher://**gopher.well.sf.ca.us**

Subject: **TELEVISION**
Description: Programme and product information

URL: gopher://**uts.mcc.ac.uk/ Gopher Services**

Subject: **THESAURUS**
Description: Project Gutenburg bring you the *Roget's Thesaurus* in its entirety
URL: gopher://**uts.mcc.ac.uk/Experimental and New Services**

Subject: **TRAINS**
Description: Oh yes indeedy, the history of trains, railways, the underground system. It's all here and waiting for Arthur Anorak to pop along
URL: ftp://**quartz.rutgers.edu/pub/railfan**

Subject: **TRAVEL**
Description: Travel information centre
URL: http://**www.explore.com**

Subject: **UFOs**
Description: Everything relating to UFO's, crop circles, odd and weird things
URL: ftp://ftp**/spies.com/Library/Fringe/Ufo**

Subject: **UNITED NATIONS**
Description: The United Nations gopher, with everything you could want to know about the, er, United Nations
URL: gopher://**gopher.undp.org**

Subject: **UNPLASTIC NEWS**
Description: An electronic magazine of the distinctly teapot variety
URL: ftp://**ftp.eff.org/pub/journals**

Subject: **VIRTUAL REALITY**
Description: Just about everything in the world of virtual reality, well virtually
URL: ftp://**milton.u.washington.edu/pub/virtual-worlds**

Subject: **VIRUSES**
Description: Lots of information about computer viruses, Internet viruses, and how to protect yourself against them
URL: gopher://**wiretap.spies.com/Wiretap On-line Library/Technical Information**

Subject: **WAIS**
Description: The Wide Area Information Server comes to the World Wide Web, and what a lot of W's that was Wavey!
URL: http://**www.wais.com/directory-of-servers.html**

Subject: **WEATHER**
Description: Various views of the weather as shown by satellite pictures, updated daily. An excellent resource
URL: ftp://**ftp.met.ed.ac.uk/pub/images/jpeg**

Subject: **WINDSURFING**
Description: A windsurfing enthusiasts mailing list
URL: mailto://**windsurfing-request@gcm.com**

Subject: **WITCHCRAFT**
Description: Lots of texts relating to all aspects of the Wicca religion
URL: ftp://**nic.funet.fi/pub/doc/occult/wicca**

Subject: **WUARCHIVE**
Description: One of the biggest Anonymous FTP sites, because of its popularity you might find it difficult to get connected to this one
URL: ftp://**wuarchive.wustl.edu**

Subject: **WWW FAQ**
Description: A Frequently Asked Questions file devoted to the World Wide Web
URL: http://**www.vuw.ac.nz:80/non-local/gnat/www-faq.html**

Subject: **WWW RESOURCE LIST**
Description: A list of places to visit on the Web, compiled and maintained by John Makulowich
URL: http://**www.clark.net/pub/journalism/awesome.html**

Chapter 9
Jargon busting

One of the things I have always found annoying when reading books on any specialist subject is that the author oftens assumes a degree of technical knowledge with regard to jargon. I don't assume, nor would I expect, that the readers of this book will be aware of every term used. Therefore, I have compiled a handy and comprehensive glossary of Internet and Comms terminology. If I have done my job properly, and there is a first time for everything, then you should be able to locate any word you are unsure of here and find its meaning.

Glossary

ACK An acknowledgement number carried in the TCP header that tells a TCP sender the sequence number of the byte which the TCP receiver expects next.

Address Either the address of a user or a system, as in an email address (required so the message sent can be directed to a particular person) or the address of a site on the Net.

AFS A set of protocols, similar to NFS, that allow for the use of files on another network machine as if they were on your local machine.

Analogue Loopback A modem self test which tests the modem's originate or answer frequency.

Analogue Signals	Continuous but varying waveforms, an example being the voice tones transmitted over a telephone line.
ANSI	American National Standards Institute, responsible for approving standards in many areas.
Anonymous FTP	Anonymous FTP allows a user to retrieve files from another site on the Internet without having to establish a userid and password on the system.
Application	A piece of software that performs a useful function.
Arc	To create a compressed archive of a file, or group of files, using the PKARC compression program. Now very dated, but many arc'ed files are still to be found on the Internet.
Archie	A system for finding publicly available files for FTP over the Internet.
Archive	A file, or group of files, that have been compressed to form one smaller file. Depending on the program used to compress the archive, it will bear one of many file extensions, including .lha .zip .arc .zoo .tar

ARPA	Advanced Research Projects Agency, part of the United States Department of Defence.
ARPAnet	The experimental network upon which the Internet was based.
ARQ	Automatic Repeat Request. An error control protocol used by Miracom modems.
ASCII	American Standard Code for Information Interchange. A code supported by just about every computer manufacturer to represent letters, numbers, and special characters.
Asynchronous	A form of data transmission which allows information to be sent at irregular intervals.
Bandwidth	The difference in Hertz between the highest and lowest frequencies of a transmission channel. Usually used to describe the amount of traffic through a particular newsgroup or conference.
Bang Path	An old UUCP EMail address system.
Barf	A failure to work!

Baseband	A digital signalling technique used in Ethernet local area networks.
Baud	Unit of measurement denoting the number of transitions in modem signal per second. Each transition may carry more than one bit of information.
BBS	Bulletin Board System.
Bigot	A common character type found in Cyberspace.
Bit	A unit of measurement that represents one character of data. A bit is the smallest unit of storage in a computer.
BITNET	An IBM-based academic computer network. BITNET is an acronym for "Because It's Time, NETwork"
Bits Per Second	The speed at which bits are transmitted.
Blinking	Using an Off Line Reader to access an online system.
Block	Data consisting of a fixed number of characters or records, moved as a single unit during transmission.
Bogus	Non-functional, or not nice.

Bounce	When email is returned due to a failure to deliver.
Bridge	A device that connects two or more physical networks and forwards packets between them.
Broadband	A transmission method often used to send different kinds of signal at the same time, like voice and data for example.
Buffer	A memory area used as a temporary storage device for data during input/output operations.
Byte	A group of binary digits that are stored and operated upon as a unit.
Cable	A bunch of insulated wires with end connectors, an example being a serial cable.
Carrier	A signal of continuous frequency capable of being modulated with another information carrying signal.
CCITT	International Consultative Committee for Telegraphy and Telephony. An organisation that produces international technical standards for data communications. Has recently been replaced by the ITU-T.

Cello A World Wide Web graphical browser program for Windows users.

Character A binary representation of a letter, number or symbol.

CIM The CompuServe Information Manager is the officially supported off line reader and system navigator for CompuServe.

CI$ See also "CIS". The dollar sign replaces the "S" in this slang version, due to the cost of using the service.

CIS CompuServe, the American online information service.

CIX Compulink Information eXchange. The largest conferencing system in the UK.

CIX The Commercial Internet Exchange, an agreement among Internet service providers regarding the commercial use of the Internet. Not to be confused with the Compulink Information eXchange although it quite often is, as they share the same acronym.

CIXen	People who use the Compulink Information eXchange.
Client	An application that extracts information from a server on your behalf.
CommUnity	The Computer Communicators' Association, set up to protect and further computer communications in the UK. Similar in aims to the EFF, but with a UK perspective.
COM	A code in MS-DOS that refers to a serial port.
Compress	A UNIX archiving program that "compresses" the size of a file.
Conference	A message area, or forum, on a conferencing system like CIX. Each conference covers a defined subject matter, and is further subdivided into topics of more specific subject matter. For example, there may be a Sooty conference which has topics of Sooty, Sweep, and Sue.
Connect Time	The length of time you spend on-line to the Internet.
Cookie	A random quote, generated by software. Found on many online systems.

CoSy	CoSy is the operating system that online services like CIX and BIX are based upon. It is a shortening of the words "Conferencing System".
CPS	Characters Per Second. A measurement of data output speed.
Crash	A sudden and total system failure.
CRC	Cyclic Redundancy Checking. A type of error detection.
CREN	The Corporation for Research and Educational Networking, which was formed by a merger of BITNET and CSNET.
Cross post	To post the same message to more than one conference, message area, newsgroup.
CTS	Clear To Send, an RS-232C signal that basically means that everything is OK for transmission of data.
Cyberpunk	A person who "lives" in the future culture of Cyberspace, Virtual Reality etc. As epitomised by the works of Bruce Sterling.
Cyberspace	A term coined by William Gibson in his novel "Neuromancer" used to

	describe the collective "World" of networked computers. Now commonly used to refer to the world that exists within computer networks, accessed by comms technology. My favourite definition is simply "the electric domain".
Daemon	A program which sits on a system waiting to perform a specific function automatically. Daemon is an acronym for "Disk and Execution MONitor".
DARPA	The Defence Advanced Research Projects Agency, responsible for the development of ARPANET which was the basis of what was to develop into the Internet.
DASD	Direct Access Storage Device.
Data Compression	The compression of information to decrease transferred file size. MNP5 and V.42bis are the best known types.
Datagram	The primary unit of information transferred over the Internet using the Internet Protocol.
DCE	Data Communications Equipment.

Decryption	Decoding encrypted data to its original form.
Dial-Up	To connect to another computer by calling it over the telephone network.
DIP Switch	Dual Interface Poll switch which enables the user to set various parameters of a circuit board (commonly found on modems and printers).
DNS	Domain Name System is a database system for translating computer domain names into numeric Internet addresses.
Domain	Part of the naming hierarchy of the Internet.
Domain Name Server	Domain Name Servers enable domain names to be resolved into numerical IP addresses.
Down	Not working, as in "the BBS is down".
Download	The transfer of a file from another, remote, computer to your computer.
DTE	Data Terminal Equipment.

DTR Data Terminal Ready, an RS-232C signal that is part of the handshake in a data transmission interface.

Duplex A communications channel capable of carrying a signal in both directions.

EARN European Academic Research Network.

EFF Electronic Frontier Foundation, an American organisation that addresses the social and legal issues arising from the increased use of computer communications.

EMACS One of the most common editors found on online systems.

Email Electronic mail. A method of sending messages via computer instead of the usual land-based postal system. One of the most popular and important uses of computer communications.

Emote Icons See "smiley".

Encryption A method of coding data to prevent unathorised access, most commonly used on the Internet to protect email from prying eyes.

Equalisation	A compensation circuit built into some modems to offset distortion caused by the telephone channel.
Error Control	A variety of different techniques which check the reliability of characters or blocks of data.
Ethernet	A type of high speed local area network.
EUNet	European UNIX Network.
FAQ	A Frequently Asked Question. You will find FAQ files all over the Internet, in Usenet Newsgroups, mailing lists, at FTP, Gopher, and WWW sites. You'll even find a FAQ section in this book!
File Server	A computer that stores files on the Internet, making them available for access by various Internet tools.
Finger	A program that displays the user, or users, on a remote system.
Firewall	A firewall is a security device to help protect a private network from Internet crackers and hackers. It is a machine with two network interfaces that is configured to restrict what protocols can be used

	across the boundaries and to decide what internal IP addresses can be seen to the external Internet.
Flame	An abusive or personal attack against the poster of a message. A flame is the online equivalent of losing your rag or thumping your teapot.
Flow Control	A technique to compensate for the differences in the flow of data input and output from a modem.
Fortune Cookie	See "Cookie".
Forum	A message area on CompuServe or Delphi,, equivalent to an echo on Fidonet, a newsgroup on USENET, or a conference on CIX.
Fragmentation	The process by which an IP datagram is broken into smaller pieces, so as to meet the requirements of a specific physical network.
Frame	A block of data with header and trailer information attached.
FreeNet	A popular method of providing "free" access to the Internet from th United States. Probably the most

	famous being the Cleveland FreeNet, which was also the first.
FTP	The File Transfer Protocol that defines how files are transferred over the Internet.
Full Duplex	Flow of information in both directions at the same time.
Gateway	A computer system to transfer data between otherwise incompatible networks.
Gibson, William	Author of "Neuromancer". Responsible for coining the term "Cyberspace".
Gopher	A menu-based system for exploring the Internet.
Hacker	Someone who enjoys exploring computer systems, often applied to people who undertake such explorations illegally.
Half Duplex	Flow of information in both directions, but one way at a time.
Handshaking	An exchange of signals allowing communication between two devices, designed to start, or keep, the two in synchronisation.

Hayes	A modem manufacturer responsible for the first direct connection modems, and whose command set has become the industry standard.
Header	Part of a packet which precedes the actual data and contains source, destination, and error checking information.
Host	A computer that allows users to communicate with other computers on a network.
Hostname	The name given to a host computer.
HST	High Speed Technology. A proprietary signalling scheme used as part of the trademark for Miracom HST modems.
HTML	HyperText Mark-up Language, the language used to write a World Wide Web document.
HTTP	HyperText Transfer Protocol, used extensively by World Wide Web. Another of the many Internet protocols.
Hub	A device connected to many other devices.

Hz	Hertz. A measurement of frequency, each unit being one cycle per second.
IAB	The Internet Architecture Board, if you like the "head honchos" who make decisions about Internet standards.
ICMP	Internet Control Message Protocol is the group of messages exchanged by IP modules in order to report errors.
Internet	Worldwide network of computer networks, connected using the IP protocol.
Internet Society	An organisation that exists to support the Internet, and also the governing body of the Internet Architecture Board.
IP	Internet Protocol on which the Internet is based.
IRC	Internet Relay Chat allows many users to chat in real time across the Internet.
ISDN	Integrated Services Digital Network combines voice and digital network services in one medium.

ISN	Initial Sequence Number is the first sequence number used on a TCP connection.
ITU-T	International Telecommunications UnionTelecommunications. The telecommunications standards making organisation, which replaces the CCITT.
JANET	The Joint Academic NETwork of educational establishments in the UK.
JUNET	Japanese UNIX Network.
KA9Q	An implementation of TCP/IP for amateur packet radio systems.
Kermit	A file transfer protocol named after Kermit the Frog!
Kernel	The system commands containing level of an operating system or network system.
Kill File	A file which filters out any messages posted by those people named in it. If someone is in your kill file, you never see any messages from them again, hence you have effectively killed them. Seen in great numbers on Usenet but also implemented in

	a growing number of Off Line Readers for various online systems.
Kit	Computer equipment.
Knowbot	The Knowbot Information Service is another method of trying to find where someone dwells within the Internet.
LAN	Local Area Network, a data network that serves a small area only.
Leased Line	A permanent connection between two sites, which requires no voltage on the line and no dialling.
LED	Light Emitting Diode. A device that emits light when electrical voltage is applied to it. Used on modem front panels as status indicators.
Line Noise	Disruption of computer communications caused by interference on the telephone line.
Lion Nose	See "line noise",
listserv	An automated mailing list distribution system.
Local Echo	All transmitted data is sent to the screen of the sending computer.

Log	A record of file operations. In comms use, the storing to disk or file of an on-line session.
Login	The process of identifying yourself on an online system. Generally a two stage process involving the input of your username followed by your password.
Login Name	The "username" or name of your account used for identification purposes.
Lurker	Someone who reads but doesn't post in newsgroups, conferences, or message areas. A sort of online voyeur.
Macro	A macro instruction is a string or instruction replaced by a shorter string or instruction. In use this means you can execute a long sequence by typing just a short one.
Mail Gateway	A machine that transfers mail between two or more EMail systems.
Mailing List	A discussion group whose messages are distributed by email.
MHS	Message Handling System.
MILNET	The US MILitary NETwork.

MIME	Multi-purpose Internet Mail Extensions, a method of linking binary code into email.
MNP	Microcom Network Protocol is a common modem error correction system.
Mode	A specific condition or state under which a device may operate.
Modem	MOdulator/DEModulator. A device to convert binary information into an analogue signal that can be transmitted over normal voice carrying telephone lines, and convert that signal back into computer readable data at the other end.
Moderator	The person who runs, or moderates, a conference or message area.
Mosaic	Probably the most commonly used World Wide Web graphical browser. Has been developed for many platforms, including Windows, Amiga, X-Windows, and Macintosh.
MTU	Maximum Transmission Unit is the largest unit of data that can be sent on a given system.

MUD	Multi User Dungeon, an online, role playing adventure game.
MUG	Multi User Game, any online game where there are two or more players at the same time.
Net	Generally used as another name for the Internet, although sometimes people refer to both Usenet and Cyberspace in general as "The Net".
Netfind	A service that helps find EMail addresses for people on the Internet.
Net God	Someone who has achieved a "Godlike" status on the Net, either through the development of part of the Net or tools used in it, or because of their presence on the Net.
Net Police	A derogatory term applied to those people who feel it is their duty to tell others how they should behave in Cyberspace.
Net Surfer	Someone who "surfs" the Internet, wandering around looking for interesting places to visit, interesting files to grab, and interesting people to talk to.

Netiquette	The supposed etiquette of the online community, examples being avoiding overuse of quoting, avoiding cross posting, and so on.
Network	A group of computers that can communicate with each other.
Newbie	Someone who is a newcomer to a Usenet group, often used as a term of ridicule or abuse.
Newsgroup	A message area, defined by subject matter, which forms part of Usenet.
NFS	The Network File System, allows use of files on remote network machines as if they were one your local machine.
NIC	Network Information Centre.
Node	A computer attached to a network.
NRAM	Non-volatile memory used by such devices as modems to store a user definable configuration which is read and acted upon at power up.
NSFNET	The National Science Foundation Network is one of the networks that makes up the Internet.

Null Modem	A cable used to directly connect two computers by their serial ports in which the transmitting and receiving pins are swapped.
Numeric Database	A database containing, specifically and unsurprisingly, numbers.
Offline	Not connected to an online system.
Off Line Reader	See "OLR".
OLR	Off Line Reader, a program that enables you to connect to an online system, download all your messages and email, read and reply to the offline and then send back your replies. An OLR can save you lots of money in telephone bills and online service charges, as well as provide, in some cases, a better user interface to the online system.
On-line	Refers to when two computers are connected by means of modems. For example, a Bulletin Board System is also an Online System.
Originate Mode	When the modem transmits in frequencies which are the reverse of the modem being called which is in answer mode.
Packet	A bundle of data.

Parity Bit	A check bit added to a unit of data for error checking purposes.
Password	A security string that is required to be input before access to a system, or part of a system, may be garnted.
Phreaking	Making phone calls while bypassing the charging system. Phone phreaking was the forerunner to hacking as we understand it today.
PING	Packet Internet Groper is a program used to test destinations on the Internet to see if they exist, are operating, etc.
Plonk	The sound a newbie makes as he plummets to the bottom of a killfile list in a Usenet group.
Pointer	A file marker so that an online system can remember what messages you have read when you disconnect, so you don't have to read them all again next time.
Polling	Connecting to another system to check for email and messages etc.
Port Number	Computers which run the TCP/IP protocols can use different ports to run different services. Each of these ports is allocated a specific

	number. Local services tend to be assigned on higher port numbers.
Post	To send a message, either by email or to a conference, message area, or newsgroup.
Postmaster	The person responsible for taking care of mail across the Internet.
PPP	Point to Point Protocol. This allows a computer to use TCP/IP with a standard telephone line.
Profile	A control file for a program. Most commonly used to set up a users individual preferences when logging onto an online service.
Protocol	Standards governing the transfer of information between computers. Developed to improve the reliability and speed of data transfer.
Public Domain	Software available to anyone without the need to pay for it.
Remote Echo	Everything the remote computer transmits is duplicated on your computer's screen.
REN	Ring Equivalent Number refers to a total figure which must not be

	surpassed by equipment connected to a single telephone socket.
REN and STIMPY	Happy Happy, Joy Joy.
Resumé	A text file containing personal information about a user of an online system, usually written by the user themselves.
RFC	Request For Comments are sets of papers used for discussion on Internet standards.
ROT-13	A simple form of encryption, commonly applied to some USENET messages, which rotates the alphabet 13 places forwards or backwards.
Router	A system that transfers information between two networks using the same protocols.
Scratchpad	A temporary file used to hold messages while awaiting transfer or editing. Used on some online systems such as CIX.
Serial Cable	The cable used to connect devices through a computer's serial port.
Serial Port	The port that transmits and receives asynchronous data. Peripheral

	devices such as modems, printers, and mice can all use the serial port.
Server	A computer, or the software on that computer, that allows other computers to use it by means of client software.
Service provider	Any organisation offering connections to the Internet, or part of it.
Shareware	Software which is generally available as "try before you buy" with the available version needing to be registered before its full power can be unleashed.
SIG	Special Interest Group, a forum or collection of forums on a particular subject. Found on on-line systems such as Delphi and CompuServe.
Signal to noise ratio	Used to describe the amount of on topic postings as compared to the amount of wibble within a message area or conference.
Signature	A personal tag line used on the end of messages posted to online services. These can vary from a couple of words to many lines long. Also known commonly as "sigs".

Site	Any of the individual networks that, as a whole, comprise the Internet.
SLIP	Serial Line IP is a protocol that allows a computer to use the Internet protocols using a standard telephone line.
Smiley	A smiling face character made by joining ASCII characters together. Used to express emotions etc. See the "Smiley Dictionary" in this book for more details.
SMTP	Simple Mail Transfer Protocol is used to transfer email between computers, as part of the TCP/IP protocol family.
Snail Mail	The sending of mail using the traditional land based postal system as opposed to email. So called because of its slowness compared to electronic mail.
Start/Stop Bits	Bits attached to a character before transmission during an asynchronous transfer.
Sterling, Bruce	Author mainly responsible for the coining of the term "Cyberpunk".
SysOp	SYStem OPerator, the person who runs a Bulletin Board System.

TCP Transmission Control Protocol, one of the protocols upon which the Internet is based.

Teapot One of my favourite words.

Teledildonics The sexual act performed with the aid of Virtual Reality, computers, telecommunications and a couple of very sad and lonely people.

Telnet An Internet protocol that allows you to login to other computer systems on the Net.

Thread A series of postings to a message area or conference that are linked together. A thread consists of an initial posting followed by all the comments to it, and forms an online conversation or debate.

Throughput The amount of data transmitted per second without the overhead of protocol information.

TLA A Three Letter Acronym, although these are often found to contain more than three letters. Used to minimise typing and speed up communications. See the "TLA Dictionary" in this book for more details.

Topic	A subdivision of a conference, where the subject matter has been more distinctly defined. See entry for "conference" for more details.
UDP	User Datagram Protocol, another of the protocols upon which the Internet is based.
UNIX	An operating system commonly used across the Internet.
Upload	The sending of a file from your computer to another, remote, computer.
URL	Uniform Resource Locator, an attempt to standardise the location or address details of Internet resources. Most commonly used, at the moment, in connection with the World Wide Web.
Usenet	A group of systems that exchange debate, chat, etc in the form of newsgroups across the Internet.
UUCP	Unix to Unix copy is used for copying files between unix systems.
UUencode	A method of encoding binary data so that it can be sent as an ASCII file across networks by email. A decoder

is required to convert the file back into an executable binary file again.

V.21 An ITU-T standard, a modem speed of 300bps

V.22 An ITU-T standard, a modem speed of 1,200bps

V.22bis An ITU-T standard, a modem speed of 2,400bps

V.23 An ITU-T standard, sending data at 75bps and receiving data at 1,200bps

V.32 An ITU-T standard, a modem speed of 9600bps

V.32bis An ITU-T standard, a modem speed of 14,400bps

V.34 An ITU-T standard a modem speed of 28,800bps

V.42 An ITU-T error correction standard

V.42bis An ITU-T error correction standard with data compression

Veronica An Internet tool that provides a Gopher menu that matched your keyword Gopher search.

Video Display	A monitor to those not talking techno-babble Terminal
Virtual Circuit	A logical transmission path.
Virtual Communities	A term that describes the communities that are very real, but exist only in computer networks. Another name for Cyberspace.
Virtual Reality	A computer technology that creates an illusion of being in an artificial world. Virtual Reality has already found its way into many real-life applications, from chemistry to architecture to games.
Virus	A program designed to infect and sometimes destroy other programs and computer equipment. Virus programmers are known, politely, as SMEEEEEEEEEEEEEEGHEADS.
WAIS	Wide Area Information Servers are used for searching databases across the Internet.
WAN	A Wide Area Network as opposed to a Local Area Network.
White Pages	A list of Internet users, accessible through the Internet itself.

Whois	An Internet program to find out the email address etc of someone froma given name.
Wibble	Nonsense posted to a message area, conference, or newsgroup. Made into an art form by the likes of talk.bizarre on Usenet and the norman conference on CIX.
World Wide Web	A hypertext-based information and resource system for the Internet.
WWW	See "World Wide Web".
X.25	A packet switched data network, which is usually half-duplex.
X.29	The command set used to configure and establish X.25 connections.
X.400	An ITU-T standard for email formats.
Zip	To archive a file or group of files using the PKZip archiver.

Index

Other Internet books from Future Publishing

This books forms part of a series of 12 Internet guides published by Future Publishing. We also publish an umbrella Internet title called 'All you need to know about the Internet', which costs £14.95 and comes with a free disk containing Chameleon Sampler, a demo suite of Internet software for PC owners.

'All you need to know about the Internet' is the perfect reference guide for newcomers to the Internet. It introduces all the activities you can engage in on the Net, including email, newsgroups, mailing lists, file transfer and much, much more.

All of these books are published in conjunction with Future Publishing's brand new UK-based .net magazine, which contains features for both experienced net users and newcomers. It features very high production and editorial quality, and is an essential source of information for those discovering the Internet's amazing potential. Retailing for £2.95, it's available at all good newsagents.

Future Publishing is committed to providing the best possible coverage of the Internet, which we believe is the computing revolution of the decade. Part of this coverage is this series of .net Guides, each targeted at specific Net users and needs. Each .net Guide consists of between 150-200 pages, is sized at 220mm (H) x 150mm (W) and retails at £7.95. Here is a list of all 12 titles:

.net Guide #1
All you need to know about Getting On-Line
by Toby Simpson
How to get on the Net quickly, easily and cheaply. No nonsense, no jargon, no hassle.
ISBN 1-898275-31-9
Publication Date November 1994

.net Guide #2
All you need to know about Communicating On-Line
by Davey Winder
Do you know 3 million people? You do now. Find out how to talk to people all over the world.
ISBN 1-898275-32-7
Publication Date November 1994

.net Guide #3
All you need to know about Using the Net
by Davey Winder
The Net software is your gateway to a world of information. Find out how to really use it.
ISBN 1-898275-33-5
Publication Date November 1994

.net Guide #4
All you need to know about Teleworking
by Gus Chandler
No commuting, no rush-hour... no boss? Find out how to work from home via the Net.
ISBN 1-898275-34-3
Publication Date November 1994

.net Guide #5
All you need to know about On-Line Information
by Gus Chandler
Forget your local library. The Net is the biggest source of information the world has ever seen. Find out how to get it.
ISBN 1-898275-35-1
Publication Date January 1995

.net Guide #6
All you need to know about Mailing Lists
by Davey Winder
Don't go searching for information – make it come to you. Keep up to date on anything from poodles to particle accelerators.
ISBN 1-898275-36-X
Publication Date January 1995

.net Guide #7
All you need to know about Setting up a BBS
by Toby Simpson
Find out how to run your own on-line service. What it costs, what to avoid – and how to make it a success.
ISBN 1-898275-37-8
Publication Date January 1995

net Guide #8
All you need to know about On-Line Gaming
by Davey Winder
Games consoles are history. Discover real gaming with real people in real situations. On-line gaming is the future.
ISBN 1-898275-38-6
Publication Date January 1995

.net Guide #9
All you need to know about UK Internet Service Providers
by Davey Winder
You need a Service Provider. Find out who offers what and for how much.
ISBN 1-898275-39-4
Publication Date January 1995

.net Guide #10
All you need to know about The World Wide Web
by Davey Winder
Compare colour TV with long-wave radio. That's the WorldWide Web compared to the standard Net interface. Believe it.
ISBN 1-898275-40-8
Publication Date January 1995

.net Guide #11
All you need to know about Business On-Line
by Davey Winder
Good business is all about communication, expertise and commercial awareness. Find out how the Net will give you the edge.
ISBN 1-898275-42-4
Publication Date February 1995

.net Guide #12
All you need to know about Internet jargon
by Davey Winder
Baffled by jargon? Hacked off with technical terms? Every Internet buzz-word is explained right here. In plain English.
ISBN 1-898275-43-2
Publication Date February 1995

To find out the latest on availability and prices, call our order hotline

☎ 01225 822511